THE POWER OF
Crystal Healing

THE POWER OF
Crystal Healing

A Complete Guide to Stone and Energy Work

BY UMA SILBEY, MASTER HEALER

MANDALA

SAN RAFAEL LOS ANGELES LONDON

To all who have taught me,
and to the Devas of Crystal and Stone
who continue to share with me
their voices.

Contents

Introduction

A WORD FROM THE AUTHOR

I have been working with stones and rocks for most of my adult life, and I have been working with crystal healing for the almost forty-five years since I picked up my first clear quartz crystal. I had been doing yoga and meditation for years at that point, living undisturbed in an ashram where I spent so much of my time meditating (between fifteen and twenty hours per day) that I needed only an hour or two of sleep at night. When I found my first crystal, or rather it found me, I was so sensitive to and immersed in the higher planes of awareness that as soon as I touched it, I felt its extremely clear vibration. I also knew exactly how to work with it, a knowledge that emerged from my deepest being and that I felt had been with me for lifetimes. Still, I wanted to learn more, so I went on to study crystal and stone healing, as well as other healing methods, with shamans and indigenous healers for many more years. The two most powerful lessons I learned from my various teachers were to trust and follow the voice within, and to follow the guidance of the stones and crystals—lessons I am now passing on to you.

Realizing the potential of crystal healing to help people live happier, more loving, and more empowered lives, I decided to offer my knowledge to everyone rather than keeping it to myself. In the late 1970s, I started teaching this ancient wisdom to whoever was receptive. I began by offering stones and crystal jewelry as tools for self-development, empowerment, and healing. In 1980, I realized that just providing stones and crystals wasn't enough: I also needed to provide accompanying information about how to work with them. As a result, I started work on my first book. I also recorded guided visualizations and meditation music to help people develop the one-pointed focus and higher awareness necessary to sense or feel the vibratory qualities of the stones. I toured around the world holding workshops and doing media appearances to teach people how to work with the stones. Since then, I have written several more books and made many more recordings so that people's knowledge of crystals could continue to grow. To this day, I continue to teach. I still have my very first crystal, the one that originally "spoke" to me. And I still do crystal and stone healings for whoever requests them, usually just in the course of my everyday life.

I say with confidence that as long as you expand your awareness, learn the basics, and listen to the crystals and stones, there is nothing that cannot be healed; however, healing may not happen the way that *you* think it should. It happens in the way that is most appropriate for the person or situation being healed, the way that the spirit or higher intelligence intends. I have learned that the most effective healing takes place when you merely set the conditions and then "get out of the way." The more that you try to force healing to happen, or make demands as to how it should happen, the more you will impede the healing process. This is one of the most important lessons that I can impart to you about crystal healing.

I have experienced and facilitated some amazing physical, mental, emotional, and spiritual healings while doing my work with crystals and stones. I have seen long-term physical impediments go away. I have seen crooked spines straighten, migraines disappear, digestive and stomach problems vanish, and frozen joints regain their flexibility. People with mental/emotional problems seem to be drawn to work with me. Coupled with traditional psychological and counseling techniques (I am formally trained), I have been able to use my stones to dissolve anxiety, evaporate the physical, mental, and emotional symptoms of stress, dissipate anger and rage, turn suicidal thoughts to acceptance, shift helplessness to personal power, and help create joy from sorrow. I have used my stones to help raise people's consciousness and increase their intuitive powers. Following the instructions in this book, you, too, can help people effect these kinds of changes in their lives. Ultimately, what you achieve with your crystal healing is limited only by your own conception of what is possible.

Even though I use the term *I* when talking about my work as a healer, I am clear that it is not my limited self that performs the healing. It is only from the limitless *I* that exists beyond body and mind, undifferentiated from the whole, that healing happens. I don't even *try* to be a crystal healer. I merely hold a healing attitude and offer myself as an instrument when, in the course of my daily life, healing opportunities present themselves. Healers of all kinds have carried this essential attitude throughout the ages. I urge you to carry this attitude yourself so that you, too, can be a successful crystal healer.

Finally, I would encourage you to be unafraid in your crystal healing work, to test your results in real life, and to forge ahead with confidence. I further encourage you to be courageous enough to let go of all preconceptions about reality and possibility, to let go of all limiting self-judgments, and to accept yourself as you are: an amazing human being in your own right. May your crystal work ultimately teach you that you are perfect as you are, that you are a valuable human being, and that you are, at your core, a beautiful soul, limitless in your light.

I BOW BEFORE YOUR LIGHT
AND THE LIMITLESS LIGHT OF THE UNIVERSE
WITHIN YOUR SOUL.
AS A CARRIER OF THE LIGHT,
MAY YOU BE A SUCCESSFUL CRYSTAL HEALER.
MAY YOU BE HAPPY AND AT PEACE.

ANCIENT SECRETS FOR MODERN TIMES

Whether you feel a special calling to perform crystal healing or are merely curious about the practice, this book was written with you in mind. It is also intended as a guide for anyone who longs to experience what lies beyond the realm of the physical senses. It is for those of you who want to contribute to the health of our planet and all its beings. When you work with crystal healing, you will find that you are able to live more expansively and with greater awareness, and you will feel a deep inner peace blossoming within. You will also gain the ability to be an effective healer. The further you progress along the crystal healing path, the more you will open to the light of the conscious wisdom that not only exists within you, but also provides the guiding intelligence that supports all life.

More often than not, those who are drawn to crystals, or choose to work with crystal healing, are those who can't help but be attracted to the stones. In other words, the crystals have "spoken" to them in one way or another. Even if a crystal just catches your eye, that in itself is a form of speaking. It is likely that all rocks, from the ordinary to the gemstone, speak to you now or have always spoken to you, not only from childhood, but also from lifetime to lifetime.

Working with crystals and crystal healing is an ancient art based on wisdom long available to sages, seers, saints, and energy healers. Today, this wisdom is equally accessible to the "ordinary" person, which means that the world and every being in it may be healed.

MATTER IS ENERGY
AND ULTIMATELY PURE BEING ITSELF.

Recognizing your own limitless existence brings a new kind of knowing, a larger awareness independent of your body or intellectual mind. This larger awareness, which is also independent of time, can best be described as a state of pure and present being. As a crystal healer, when you are centered in this pure state, the universe, or life itself, will speak to you as a river of knowledge endlessly flowing within. This is the secret that mystics, spiritualists, healers, saints and sages have known throughout the ages. The more you center your attention to this "voice" within your being, the more you will gain the ability to "hear." Working with crystal healing in the way this book instructs will teach you how to listen so that you can become aware of the knowledge you already possess.

When you are aware and centered in the present, your rocks will guide you in your work. The more you listen, the more you will know what to do without having to refer to outside material, except maybe as a starting point. Though this book will present a great deal of important information, much of which stems from the most ancient of times, ultimately your success as a crystal healer will depend on your ability to hear your stones.

In the course of your crystal work, the river of knowledge within will reveal itself to you in many different ways. You may hear it with your inner ear, see it with your mind's eye, feel it physically, or just sense it. No matter how you experience this knowledge, once you are able to hear the rock or crystal, you will know what to do with it in every moment, in every situation, with every person, and in every environment. The correct path will be completely obvious to you at all times. Because the ability to hear the voice of the stones is the basis of the most effective crystal healing work, the more you can be present-centered and listen, the better healer you will be. In the pages of this book, you will discover ancient and modern techniques designed to help you stay grounded in the present. The more you practice these techniques, the more effortlessly you will be able to center your attention in the here and now.

Space, planets, and our earth are not the only entities made of vibration: so, too, is everything in existence. This includes your thoughts and feelings. It also includes all physical bodies, plants, minerals, sound, color, subtle bodies, auras, and objects. Each one of your crystals and stones vibrates in a particular pattern. Every type of illness or disease has a particular vibrational pattern. There is nothing in existence that is not vibratory at its core. This book will help you learn exactly how to sense or feel these patterns so you can work with them.

The essence of crystal healing, then, is to be able to sense, intuit, or feel essential vibrational patterns and use your stones to change them in ways that bring healing. Generally, this means offering yourself as an instrument of healing, using your focused intention and skill to bring a disharmonious vibrational pattern back into harmony. This method allows healing to happen in the way that is natural and best for the one being healed. *The Power of Crystal Healing* offers easy instructions, meditations and other practices to help you become the ultimate instrument of healing.

You will also learn when and how to use the many types of crystals in order to change specific vibrational patterns. You will learn how to hear and align yourself with the universal higher intelligence or spirit in order to do your work. As the ancient Wise Ones can attest, with knowledge, awareness, focus, clear intention, humility, practice, and patience, crystal healing is not hard to do.

INTELLIGENT MIND

To gain an idea of the expansive power and possibility of crystal healing work, try the following exercise: First, hold a crystal or any stone in your hand and gaze at it, then consider or "sense" the millions of years that this stone has existed. Perhaps it came into being with the very birth of the planet. Take a moment to feel the vastness of time and space that this stone or crystal represents.

Now, contemplating this stone or crystal further, realize that it is part of the mountain or cave where you found it, part of the earth's crust, and part of the earth itself, which is in fact a huge, multilayered rock. The space through which the earth and its fellow planets travel is a vast plasma composed of ions and electrons, which further devolve into magnetic fields and electrical currents unbounded by time and space.

Now, let your mind travel inward as you consider the following: All matter—including your body, the stone or crystal, the earth, the planets, and the plasma of space itself—is composed of increasingly smaller particles such as atoms, protons, neutrons, electrons, gluons, and neutrinos. Just as the planets float within a seemingly infinite space, these smaller particles are held within a minigalaxy of which space is the major component. Furthermore, whether we contemplate the infinity of matter in space, or its infinite molecular contraction, it is clear that there exists far greater space than matter. This is true for the cells and particles of your own body just as it is true for the cells and particles of the stone and the earth.

No matter how small the observed particle, it ultimately loses its dimension and solidity and becomes mere patterns of vibration and rhythm. Ultimately, then, there is nothing in our bodies or in the world around us that we would consider to be solid; there are only dynamic patterns continually being born and dying, changing forms from one to another, in a cosmic and ever-lasting dance of pure energy. Every body or form, no matter how large or small, is ultimately an expression of a particular vibrational pattern. These vibrational patterns are what we call the energy that crystal healers learn to sense and manipulate in order to affect a healing.

The crystal healer, mystic, spiritualist, quantum physicist, metaphysician, saint, and sage intuitively understand the cosmic vibrational patterns and fundamental rhythms of the universe to be a function of an underlying intelligent mind, consciousness, or spirit. Infinite and omnipresent, this essential spirit not only is at the heart of your own physical existence, but also *is* the heart of your own being. As it is limitless, so, too, are you. With expanded awareness, you can align yourself with this essential spirit or intelligent mind and successfully do your work. This book will tell you how.

ALL FORM IS SPACIOUS
AND EMPTY OF SOLIDITY.
THIS KNOWLEDGE IS KEY.

Chapter 1
ON CRYSTALS AND STONES

Though rocks and stones are often referred to as crystals, they are actually quite different. Basically, crystals are minerals; rocks and stones are not. Rocks are formed from minerals or crystals. Unlike a crystal, rocks do not have a uniform internal structure, instead appearing as a solid, naturally occurring mass. Furthermore, though all crystals are minerals, not all minerals are crystals. The mineral rose quartz, for example, rarely appears as a crystalline structure. Nor does jade or jadeite. In most cases, both of these stones are technically minerals, not crystals.

Through ancient geologic forces of time, heat, water, and pressure, a crystal grows as a three-dimensional network of atoms that are arranged in a symmetrical, repetitive pattern spiraling outward from an original "seed." This growth determines a crystal's outward shape as well as its physical properties. Furthermore, each crystalline structure varies depending on certain impurities, mineral saturations, and the temperature of the environment during its formation. These factors determine the crystal's final shape and color, and shape and color determine how the healer can use the crystal energetically.

A ROCK OR STONE IS NOT A CRYSTAL.
CRYSTALS ARE MINERALS.
NOT ALL MINERALS ARE CRYSTALS.

Though crystals, rocks, and minerals all have energy and can be used for healing, they are used differently for different reasons. Crystals are generally more versatile and powerful healing tools than rocks and noncrystalized minerals. This is because their structure and formation allow them to direct energy. Because a crystal's lattice formation extends in an outward direction from its original seed, its energy flow also extends outward. A crystal with a single termination or point, for example, has an energy flow that moves in one direction from the bottom through the tip. A double terminated crystal has a subtle energy flow moving in two directions through each of its points. Likewise, a crystal cluster's energy flow moves outward in the direction of each of its points.

The direction of the energy flow is important because, when you are working with crystal healing, you can combine your focused intention with this natural energy flow to direct energy accordingly.

When a crystal or stone has a natural termination or point, the crystal healer will have no trouble determining the direction its energy takes; however, when a crystal has been worked—either carved into a round sphere or any other shape—the natural location and direction of its original termination is disguised, making it difficult, if not impossible, to direct its energy flow. When you can't sense a crystal's energy flow, you might try to steer its energy in one direction only to end up energetically fighting with an opposing force bent on drawing the energy in another direction. There are ways to combine the carved crystal with another terminated crystal (usually clear quartz crystal) to force an energy direction, but it's not an easy task.

Crystals carved into round, oval, square, or other cabochon shapes also disguise their natural subtle energy flow. Similarly, chunks or pieces of crystal that have been carved into the traditional crystal shape, an act that interferes with their natural energy flow, are hard to direct or manipulate energetically. This is not to say that it cannot be done, but the process requires much more concentration and powered intention.

It is often the case, however, that you don't need to steer the subtle energy flow in a particular direction to do your work. This is true, for example, if you are using the color properties of the stone to influence the subtle body's response, as you would do when laying stones on the body. You may also want to do specific work with a shape that steers energy in a direction suggested by the carving—for example, when you are working with a crystal ball for divination and gazing. In this case, the roundness of the sphere easily gathers your energy into its center, allowing you to begin gazing. Different crystal shapes may also be used to create certain states of mind or empowerment. For example, a crystal cross may be used to create Christ consciousness. Carved crystal or stone animals may be used to bring the power of the represented animal to you. A pyramid may be used to send messages. A heart shape may be used to help bring you love, compassion, and empathy, whereas a diamond shape may help bring good fortune.

Though this book is specifically geared toward working with crystals in your healing, rocks also have their uses. Granite, for example, may help bring you strength. Obsidian can help bring you grounding and power, whereas white marble can be soothing. Some rocks are not actually rocks at all and can still be used for healing, usually by accessing their color properties or natural origin. Coral, for example, originally a sea creature, may bring the qualities of the ocean to your healing and is useful for its red, orange, pink, or white color. Amber, which is fossilized tree resin, can bolster your healing work through its natural qualities and its soothing yet vitalizing color.

Clear quartz crystal is the most important stone to use in your crystal healing work. It is the most versatile of all the crystals. *In fact, there is not anything you can do with a colored or other crystal or stone that you cannot do with a simple, clear quartz crystal.* Clear quartz is the most energetically powerful of all the crystals, so it can be used to amplify any other type of energy or power. You can use it to amplify the transformative power of color or colored stone. You can use it to amplify the power of thought, feeling, or visualization. You can use it to empower intention and one-pointed focus. You can use it to amplify or raise energy to help alleviate fatigue or increase personal power. You can use it to send, receive, raise, lower, cut through, or remove subtle energy in any desired direction. You can use it to send messages for long-distance healing. You can program it to act as if it is any color or colored stone, thus eliminating the need to have every different colored stone for every healing occasion. It can be employed to open, close, or balance any chakra or energy center. The use of the clear quartz crystal is limited only by the strength of your intention, your ability to focus, and your imagination.

There are four types of clear quartz crystal. The first is a natural crystal left just as it was when it was first mined from the earth. It contains all of the information and power of its time in the earth. Because our earth is a star spinning through space, you can access interplanetary information with it. The second type is a natural crystal that has been cut and polished. This carving and polishing can interfere with the original earth energies embedded in the crystal. On the other hand, the polishing can remove an opaque surface to reveal the clarity of what lies underneath. Furthermore, if the direction of the subtle energy flow is maintained, the crystal can be carved into multiple faces beyond the original six to enhance its innate power. The third type is a crystal that was grown in the lab, sometimes called *lab quartz*. Though this quartz lacks the power and information gained from thousands of years spent in the earth, it still possesses and responds to the piezoelectric energy that natural quartz gains from the eons of stress and heat involved in its formation. Even so, it is generally not as powerful as natural quartz because of its more recent creation. The fourth type of crystal is a very pretty glass that significantly, if not totally, lacks the power of natural or even lab-grown crystal. Compared to either a natural or lab-grown quartz crystal, this glass crystal is dull and not at all energetically alive. Often found in inexpensive jewelry, it *may* have some placebo effect.

The size of the crystal is not as important as its clarity. Generally speaking, the clearer the quartz crystal, the more powerful it is. This is one of the main reasons Herkimer diamonds are so potent. A type of quartz crystal that is found exclusively in Herkimer, New York, these diamonds are perhaps the most brilliant and powerful of all crystals. In addition to the size and clarity of a quartz crystal, it is important that the tip be intact. A crystal with a chipped tip will not channel energy as well as one that is whole.

As you work with crystal healing, you will likely find that the basic information about crystals (with the exception of the inefficacy of glass crystals) does not hold true in every instance. There really are no black-and-white rules, only guidelines that tend to be useful in most cases. For example, I spent more than twelve years working with a Native American medicine man, or shaman, who was an incredibly powerful and effective healer. Among his healing methods was the use of the clear quartz crystal. When he showed me his quartz crystal, I saw that it was small,

opaque, and had a chipped tip. According to traditional crystal teachings, this crystal should not have been at all suitable for healing. However, coupled with other healing methods, he did some of the most effective work with this crystal that I have ever witnessed, healing conditions ranging from heart problems to cancer.

The lesson here: Once you've thoroughly learned and explored the techniques of crystal healing, it isn't enough simply to use the tools you imagine will work best; you need to find what *actually* works for you. Moreover, what works one time with one person or in one situation will not necessarily work again in the same circumstances. Nor is a crystal that worked for one healing guaranteed to work for a second similar healing. This is true because every time you pick up your stone or crystal to do a healing, you are different, the stone or crystal is different, the person you are working with is different, and the environment is different. To be a good crystal healer, then, you need to be completely present so that you can hear what your stones are saying in any given moment. Again, listen to your stones and be willing to be spontaneous in your work. Trust yourself and your inner guidance, and you will do a good job every time.

NO CRYSTAL IS THE SAME EVERY TIME YOU USE IT.
NOR DOES IT ALWAYS DO THE SAME THING.
A GOOD CRYSTAL HEALER
IS SPONTANEOUS IN EACH MOMENT.

CENTERING AND GROUNDING

In order to sense, feel, or hear your crystals, you will need to be centered and grounded, at least while you do your crystal healing. *Grounding* means that your energy is anchored in the earth. The more grounded you are, the more energy you will have to expand your awareness into the higher planes of consciousness required to work with the subtle energy of the crystals and of the person you are seeking to cure.

You also need to be grounded in order to strengthen your subtle and physical nervous systems. When you practice crystal healing, you channel large amounts of subtle energy through your physical and subtle bodies, drawing from your etheric and physical nervous system. If you draw more from your nervous system than it is able to handle, it will become exhausted, and you will "burn out." When this happens, you might become short of temper, physically exhausted, emotionally overwrought, and unable to concentrate. Dark thoughts may cloud your mind. You may suffer from headaches, a stiff neck, uncontrollable shaking, clenched teeth, and a locked jaw. Your insight and expanded awareness will become compromised or may even disappear entirely.

If you notice these or other symptoms, it is important to pause and make sure you are properly grounded. If you do not have the physical, mental, emotional, or subtle strength to perform your crystal healing, then stop for the time being. Don't be afraid to say no. If you attempt to heal others when you are at less than full capacity, you risk attracting any negativity you release during the healing, and the healing itself is likely to be shallow and/or unsuccessful.

When you are grounded, it is easier to become centered within yourself. To be *centered* is to have your awareness entirely focused on the present moment. When you are present, your mind stops wandering, and it becomes easy to concentrate. Without this type of one-pointed focus, you will not have the sensitivity required to perform crystal healing, and your work will ring hollow at best. Grounding and a strong nervous system will help you to remain centered.

Centering and grounding alone can provide a deep healing experience. If you are working with anxiety, fear, PTSD, and symptoms of stress, sometimes the best way to affect a healing is to become grounded enough to relax. It is easy to alleviate stress and anxiety when thoughts are focused on the present, where these conditions do not exist.

You will find grounding and centering techniques later in this book, specifically in the sections related to grounding stones, one-pointed concentration, and strengthening the nervous system.

YOUR ETHERIC ROOTS INTO THE EARTH
FEED YOU STRENGTH
AND SOOTH YOUR BODY, MIND, AND FEELINGS.

FEELING CRYSTAL ENERGY

In order to work with crystal healing, you need to know how to sense, feel, and hear the energy of your crystals so that they can direct your healing work. Grounding and centering help you maintain concentrated focus and are important first steps on the path to feeling the energy of the crystals. To the extent that your attention is scattered, you will find yourself unable to connect with the energy of your stones.

Being able to feel and hear your crystals will bring you much better results than just memorizing information about them because, though stones do have certain tendencies, they seldom perform exactly the same way twice. In short, they only *tend* to have certain effects. It is infinitely better to be able to have an actual moment-to-moment experience with your stones because then you will know exactly what to do with a particular crystal as you use it. Memorization relies on the logical part of your mind. In contrast, the ability to hear your stones relies on a higher intelligence derived from an expanded awareness.

Before you learn how to feel the energy of your crystals, it is important to learn about energy fields themselves so that you will be able to understand what we mean by crystal *energy*. Everything in physical manifestation is an expression of an energy field with a certain vibratory pattern and quality. This is true whether the physical manifestation appears as an object, a human body, an emotion, or a thought. This vibratory field, however, is not solely contained within the physical manifestation but rather extends outward from it. The energy field of a physical object or human body, for example, doesn't stop at the perceived edges of the object or body. Instead, it extends outward in a surrounding vibratory aura.

Similarly, in addition to being an expression of a particular energy pattern, a thought or emotion also creates another related energy pattern. This new pattern carries out beyond the initial emotional expression or thought into the surrounding vibratory universe to affect its overall pattern. The stronger and more focused an emotion or thought is, the further outward it maintains its original form. Another way to say this is that emotions and thoughts tend to create other associated emotions and thoughts, each holding less force and creating less impact the further its extension. Eventually, the original pattern becomes indistinguishable from the total vibratory field.

This same truth holds with respect to a quartz crystal. Its surrounding energy field is part of a larger vibratory field, and so by combining the vibrations of thought, emotion, and movement with the crystal, we can change the larger vibrational field. What is changed within the larger vibrational field will, in turn, result in changes in all parts of the vibrational field, whether these parts are physical objects, human bodies, or other emotions or thoughts.

The stronger the energy your crystal has, the larger the energy field it projects. However, the clear quartz crystal, depending on certain qualities that it may or may not possess, is typically the energetically strongest of all the crystals. Generally speaking, the clearer your quartz crystal, the stronger the energy it projects and the larger the energy field that surrounds it. It seems logical to think that a larger crystal will be stronger, but this is not necessarily so. Again, clarity is much more important than size. The energy fields of your crystals can be increased with your focused intention. You can also pair two or more crystals so that their combined energy results in a larger and more powerful energy field. Similarly, crystals can be arranged in patterns, grids, or matrixes to alter their energy field so that they will be more effective in certain healings. Clearing and charging your crystals also tends to increase their energy field.

As you learn to physically feel the clear quartz crystal's subtle energy, you will find that the healing energy centered in the middle of your hands automatically begins to open, making you more and more physically sensitive to all subtle energy fields. Ultimately, you will be able to feel the energy fields of any stone or crystal, any person, animal, or plant, and any object, either from a distance or close up. Finally, the greater your feel for a crystal's energy field, the more accurately you will be able to use and direct its effects in any given healing situation. This, of course, makes your healing work very powerful.

The following instructions offer a good method for feeling the energy of your quartz crystal.

FEELING CRYSTAL ENERGY

1. After centering and grounding yourself, begin to quickly rub your palms together. As you do this, focus on the heat that builds between your hands. If your attention wanders, just bring it back to the rubbing of your hands.

2. Once your hands are quite warm, remain focused while picking up a single terminated clear quartz crystal in your right hand. Holding your left palm upward, gently touch the tip of the crystal to its center. Focus on the feeling of the crystal touching your left palm.

3. Now, while maintaining your focus on the feeling of the crystal touching your left palm, slowly pull the tip of the crystal about an inch away from your left hand. See if you can still feel a slight buoyancy, tingling, or breeze between the crystal and your palm. If you don't feel anything, put the crystal down and start over. Repeat the process until you feel a connection between the crystal and your palm.

4. Once you feel a tingling, breeze, or buoyancy, retain your concentration while you try circling the crystal around the center point of your palm in larger and larger spirals. This will help open the healing centers in your palms.

5. Next, develop your ability to feel energy fields from a distance. While maintaining the connection between your palm and the crystal, lift the crystal away from your hand another inch or so, seeing if you can still feel its presence. As long as you can feel this connection, continue raising the crystal farther away from your palm. With practice, you will be able to separate the crystal a full arm's length from your palm. With more practice, you will be able to feel your crystal from the opposite side of a room, and from even greater distances than that.

Once you can feel your crystal's energy in this way, further practice will enable you to feel the vibrational energy field of any other object, including the human body, from any distance.

BEING ABLE TO FEEL SUBTLE ENERGY FIELDS
IS ESSENTIAL IN CRYSTAL HEALING.

Chapter 2
HOW CRYSTAL HEALING WORKS

Imbalance—whether physical, mental, or emotional—is the root cause of all disease. Every physical, mental or emotional imbalance is reflected as a vibrational imbalance. Not only does physical imbalance cause a corresponding vibrational imbalance, but the vibrational imbalance in turn alters the original physical imbalance. Furthermore, this vibrational imbalance can create other compensating vibrational imbalances, which can cause imbalances of their own in a potentially endless and escalating spiral.

Because everything on the physical plane is in its essence vibration and all vibration is inextricably interrelated, *what is changed on a vibrational level will result in changes to the physical.* This is true of the physical body, the mind, and the emotions. Just as a doctor or psychologist works to create a rebalancing on a mental, emotional, or physical level, the crystal healer works to re-establish an original balance on a deeper vibrational level. In other words, the crystal healer looks past the obvious physical, mental, and emotional symptoms to sense the inner state of vibrational imbalance, then uses his or her crystals to create a state of vibrational harmony.

The placebo effect linking expectation and confidence with actual physical healing has long been affirmed. In other words, if you expect to be healed and have confidence that it will happen, your symptoms will tend to get better or heal completely, depending on the condition.

THE MIND IS A POWERFUL HEALER.
WHAT YOU EXPECT WILL LIKELY HAPPEN.

In crystal healing work, then, you use your crystals to manipulate the placebo effect and create a stronger connection between the brain and body, encouraging them to work together toward healing. At the same time, you use your crystals to shift the vibrational field from one that supports illness and disease to one that supports healing. In other words, you change the thoughts as well as the subtle vibrations.

It is important to realize that before you can create harmony within a vibrational field for someone else, you first have to create a harmonious vibrational field for yourself. If you have scattered and/or negative thoughts and feelings, if your breathing is shallow or fast, and if you are not present-centered and calm, your vibrational field will be disturbed; from such a place of disturbance, you will be unable to create harmony in another. The difference between a harmonious vibrational field and a disharmonious one is like the difference between a calm sea and one raging with waves. Just as it is difficult to hold a course in a raging sea, it is difficult to focus in the single, one-pointed direction required for crystal healing when your mind is disturbed.

Clearing and calming the vibrational field that surrounds and contains your physical body, thoughts, and emotions is one way to come back to a state of harmony and ensure that you feel balanced enough to do your healing work. If you are feeling in any way disharmonious before you begin, then take time to clear and calm your aura. It is vital that your subtle energy be balanced and free to flow unimpeded through your body, bringing you the sensitivity needed for effective healing.

Similarly, it is important to clear and balance the subtle energy field of the person you are healing before you get to work. The healing energy must be able to flow unimpeded through your subject's subtle body as well. Actually, sometimes clearing and calming the vibrational field is all that is needed in order to heal. The following instructions explain how to do this.

CALMING THE VIBRATIONAL FIELD WITH CRYSTALS

1. Hold a clear quartz crystal, preferably double terminated, in each hand. (Double terminated crystals are those with a point on each opposing end.) With your hands in your lap, standing straight or sitting upright in a chair, close your eyes. Bring your attention to your breathing and begin to take long, deep, gentle breaths. Avoid straining or gasping in any way.

2. Now, imagine that your breath flows in and out of your heart chakra in the middle of your chest. Take at least seven long, deep breaths in and out of your heart chakra.

3. After seven deep breaths in and out of your heart chakra, imagine that each inhale flows into your heart center and each exhale flows outward through the bottoms of your feet, grounding you deeply into the earth. Do this for at least seven deep breaths.

4. Now, breathe normally and begin to activate your palms and crystals with the rubbing technique taught earlier. (With practice you will be able to feel the energy of your crystals as soon as you pick them up and won't need to repeat the rubbing activation process.)

5. Now, without dropping your focus from your stones, hold one double terminated clear quartz crystal in your left hand to empower your focus and sensitivity. Hold the other double terminated crystal in your activated right hand so that you can be sensitive to the subtle vibration of the body and its surrounding vibrational field.

6. Next, take long, gentle breaths as you slowly sweep your right hand and crystal down your body about six inches from its surface, as if you are smoothing the vibrational field or aura. Start from the top of your head and slowly move down to your chest. Then gently and carefully sweep down each arm to your fingertips. Then continue sweeping down your torso to the tips of your toes. When possible, sweep the back of your body as well as the front.

7. If you feel any agitation or excitation as you pass over any part of your body, continue sweeping that area until it calms.

8. Once you are finished, hold both crystals with your arms down to your sides and your palms facing forward in receptive mode. Listen to any inner guidance that may come to you. Remain in this harmonious and receptive mode until you feel complete.

9. Now, slowly open your eyes and put your crystals down. Maintain this state of harmony, calm, clarity, and focus. Be sure to clear your crystals of any negative energy they may have acquired in the sweeping process.

If you are working with your crystals to heal another person, it is important that you do this initial sweeping with them before you start any other part of your healing process.

USE YOUR STONES TO CREATE HARMONY
AND HEALING WILL FOLLOW.

BENEFITS OF CLEAR AND COLORED CRYSTALS

As you have just learned, crystals work by creating changes in the subtle energy field in order to influence the physical world. A clear quartz crystal is the most effective crystal for this process. This is not only because of its extremely high and consistent rate of energy, but also because it can be precisely manipulated with the focused intention of your mind to make powerful changes in energy fields with which it is put in contact.

The clear quartz crystal's high vibratory rate allows you to raise your body's vibratory rate when you couple the two together. This increased vibratory rate energizes your body and mind, uplifting your feelings and thought patterns. Because illness or disease lowers your vibratory rate, using a clear quartz crystal to raise it can in itself be quite healing.

A clear quartz crystal can be programmed with any influence. For example, it can be programmed with sound, thought, visualization, scent, plants and flowers, the moon, the sun, the planets, oceans and streams, color, and anything else in the manifest universe. Afterwards, it will behave as though it actually is the influence with which you programmed it, and affect you accordingly. A clear quartz crystal programmed with the peaceful, expansive, and feminine qualities of a full moon, for example, will invest you with these same qualities. With the right programming, a clear quartz crystal will assume the healing powers of any colored crystal. More simply, a clear quartz crystal can be programmed with color alone in order to perform specific color-related healing work. If you want to cool a high fever, for example, you can program a clear quartz crystal to act as a cooling green color. The only limit to the possibilities of this pairing and programming is your own imagination and strength of focus.

More limited in scope, a colored crystal or stone will change a given vibratory rate in accordance with its innate qualities. A red jasper, for example, will raise the vibratory rate of the first chakra and bring feelings of security and strength to the physical body. Lacking the versatility of clear quartz, it cannot be programmed to act as if it is another color. You can, however, increase the power of a colored crystal by pairing it with a clear quartz crystal. If you place an emerald on the heart chakra, for example, you can increase its power by surrounding it with clear quartz crystals.

You can cause a clear crystal or colored stone to exercise certain vibrational influences just by placing it on or very near the body. However, the most powerful vibrational changes occur when this placement is accompanied with a one-pointed, focused intention governed by your strength of will. The more powerful your focus, the greater the vibrational changes you will create. The more you focus, the more you increase the energy flow of the stones and crystals.

In addition to increasing the power of the energy flow entering your body or mind, focused intention can be used to direct that energy to a specific destination. The more precise the energy flow, the more precise your healing. A specific healing requires a specific focus, so the more you can direct your mind to focus without wavering, the more likely it is that your intention will become a reality. Focus is vitally important to crystal healing work.

Certain crystals will help increase your ability to focus. First, because focus takes energy, any yellow crystals placed about two inches above your belly button will help to energize your subtle or physical nervous system, thus bringing you the increased willpower needed to focus. Red and orange crystals combined with yellow crystals will provide further energizing effects.

Besides having a strong willpower, you must be able to hold your mind steady in order to manipulate the subtle vibration of your crystals as they do their work. You can use crystals to train your mind so that it remains focused on a single point, allowing you to perform precise healings.

In order to successfully manipulate your crystals so that you are able to make the energetic changes you intend, you need to sense, feel, or harmonize yourself with them. If you are in harmony with your crystals, you will know what they are "telling you" to do, and you will easily discern where you should place them or how you should direct them. If you are unable to work with energetic focus and still try to direct energy or manipulate your crystals, you may use them in ways that are inappropriate for the intended healing. In that case, your results will be mixed at best, completely ineffective at worst.

The following are some crystal practices and meditations that you can do to increase the strength of your one-pointed focus and your willpower. The following crystal layout is intended for situations in which more subtle or physical nerve strength is needed.

CRYSTAL LAYOUT TO INCREASE NERVE STRENGTH AND WILLPOWER

1. Lie on your back on any surface you find comfortable. Be sure that your spine and body are straight. Your legs and feet should be uncrossed and parallel to each other.

2. Surround yourself with either four or eight single terminated clear quartz crystals, their tips pointing toward your body. Place one above your head, one below your feet, and one on each side of your body directly across from each other. This will surround your body in an energizing and protective aura. It will also increase the power of the other stones in this layout.

3. Place a yellow citrine, yellow quartz, or yellow jade on your abdomen about two inches above your navel point or belly button. If the crystal is terminated, point the tip toward your feet for grounding.

4. Next, place an orange aventurine or carnelian on your belly about two inches below your navel point or belly button. If the crystal is terminated, point the tip toward your feet.

5. Now place a red garnet and a ruby or red jasper below the base of your spine. If the crystal is terminated, point the tip downward, away from the bottom of your spine.

6. Next, hold both hands, palms facing upward, in Surya Ravi Mudra (a hand position) with your ring fingers touching your thumbs and your other fingers extended. Besides increasing the effects of this practice, this mudra also increases nerve strength, bringing the vitalizing energy of the sun. To increase the benefits of this mudra, place a small clear quartz crystal in each palm. If the crystals are single terminated, point the tips up toward your arms. This will help channel the energy of the mudra into your subtle and physical bodies.

7. Now that you are in position, close your eyes. Begin to take long, deep, gentle breaths in and out of your nose, completely filling and emptying your lungs without gasping. Do this until you feel calm and centered, then focus on the red crystal at the bottom of your spine. Imagine that your breath is flowing in and out of this crystal and the bottom of your spine. Imagine that the red crystal glows brighter with every inhale as its energy flows up your spine to fill your body. With every exhale, release any tension you feel in your body. Do this for at least seven full breaths.

8. Next, shift your attention to the orange crystal on your belly. Imagine that your long, deep, breaths begin to flow in and out of this orange crystal as it glows brighter with every breath. Imagine the orange from this crystal moving into your belly, filling your body with its energy with every inhale. With every exhale, let your body relax, especially your pelvic area and stomach. Do this for at least seven full breaths.

9. Now, shift your attention to the yellow crystal just above your navel point, or belly button. Imagine your breath is flowing in and out of this yellow crystal, and see the yellow color filling your navel area and abdomen with every inhale. With every exhale, let go of any tension in your body, especially in your belly and the small of your back. Continue this for at least three minutes.

10. Next, imagine that with every inhale and exhale the golden light filling your body flows outward to surround it with a glowing aura that extends as far as you can see. Imagine yourself floating within the center of a glowing field of endless sunlight. Remain in this state for at least three minutes, but feel free to continue for as long as you like. When you are finished, imagine this golden light being pulled back into your body, centering in your belly and abdomen.

11. Shift your attention back to your breathing, feeling it flow in and out of your nose. Feel the surface beneath you. When you are ready, slowly open your eyes. Release the hand mudras and reverse the placement of the crystals on either side of you. Now that you are finished, try to maintain the energy of this practice.

Besides building subtle and physical nerve strength to help you focus, this stone layout and meditation will help increase your overall energy level. It will help counteract depression and fatigue, and it will build your sense of personal power. It will increase your self-discipline, strength of mind, and willpower.

CRYSTAL MEDITATION FOR ONE-POINTED FOCUS

This crystal meditation practice will help you control the direction of your thoughts and stop them from wandering. With a strong focus, you will be able to discern and manipulate subtle energy in the way that crystal healing work requires. In order to focus your mind, you first need it to be calm. Because the breath and the mind are intimately connected, slowing and calming your breath will in turn slow and calm your thoughts. Once your thoughts are calm, you can focus them on one point.

1. Sit upright with your spine straight and eyes closed.

2. Place your hands in your lap while holding them in Hasta Hakini Mudra, a hand position that increases concentration. To do this, spread your fingers slightly apart and touch the tips of each finger to their counterparts on the other hand. Pointing the fingers slightly downward, hold a double terminated quartz crystal between your palms.

3. Begin to take long, slow, gentle breaths, completely filling and emptying your lungs. Imagine your breath flowing into your heart center in the middle of your chest with each inhale; imagine it flowing out through the bottom of your spine and into the ground with each exhale.

4. Draw your attention away from any physical sensations, thoughts, or feelings, and direct it back to your breath. Concentrate on your breath as it flows in and out of your heart chakra.

5. Practice this exercise for at least ten minutes, but feel free to continue for as long as you like.

The ability to focus with a strong subtle and physical nervous systems will not only help you with your crystal healing work, it will also help you elsewhere in your life. If your nervous system is strong, it will help protect you from anxiety, bring strength during emergencies, and bring clear mindedness in any situation. It will increase your concentration, memory, decision-making ability, mental power, personal power, and energy.

THE MAIN SUBTLE ENERGY SYSTEM

Crystal healing works with the subtle energy system as well as with the subtle body. Even if you are working to heal a specific symptom in the physical body, it will have its root in the subtle body and energy system, so if you know this system well you can work with it directly in your crystal healing.

The subtle energy system is like the bones and nerves of our physical body. All subtle energy information is transported through energy channels called *nadis* that work to direct and transfer energetic vibrations through the subtle body, much like veins and arteries carry blood through our physical body. The most basic component of this subtle energy system is a central, vertical cord of subtle energy that runs through our spine. This vertical column of subtle energy, called the *sushumna*, connects and empowers each of the seven chakras, or subtle energy centers, with subtle energy currents that extend upward from the seventh chakra on the crown and downward from the sacral, or first chakra, near the base of the spine. Also moving up the central energy cord are two other intertwining cords of energy called the *ida* and *pingala*. The ida, located on the left side of the central cord, channels feminine, moon, yin mental energy into our subtle body, stimulating the right side of the brain. The pingala, located on the right side of the sushumna, channels masculine, solar, yang energy, stimulating the left side of the brain and bringing vital energy. Beginning with the first chakra, these energy currents alternate from left to right as they move up the sushumna. As this subtle energy is free to rise up the central cord without blockages when stimulating each chakra, it will eventually flow outward from our crown chakra to expand our consciousness into the upper realms. Because each chakra is related to a different part of the body and a different mental and emotional state, blockages negatively affect your mind, emotions, and physical health. Here is a brief explanation of each chakra and its related attributes.

Located at the base of the spine, the **first chakra**, called the muladhara or sacral chakra, has a red color and is associated with basic survival. Blockages here result in problems with the bones, feet, legs, colon and elimination, weight gain, fearfulness, and overall weakness in the physical body.

The **second chakra**, roughly three inches below the navel, is orange in color and is associated with manifestation and sexuality. When this chakra is blocked, issues may include low libido or hypersexuality, emotional coldness, and reproductive or urinary tract problems.

The **third chakra**, yellow in color and located roughly two inches above the navel, is associated with vitality, willpower, and nerve strength. Blockages here tend to result in physical exhaustion, digestive problems, hypertension, adrenal issues, diabetes, allergies, lack of confidence, and various forms of dominating behavior.

The **fourth chakra**, or heart chakra, located in the middle of the chest, is related to love, compassion, and empathy. Blockages here result in problems with the heart or lungs, asthma, respiratory illnesses, and emotional issues like loneliness and a lack of deep connection with others.

The **fifth chakra**, located in the middle of the throat, is related to communication and the glandular system. Blockages here result in issues with the neck and shoulders, the throat, and the thyroid gland, as well as problems of self-expression and deceptiveness.

The **sixth chakra**, or **third eye**, located in the middle of the forehead between the brows, is related to intuition, psychic abilities, and the pineal gland. Blockages here may bring headaches and migraines, vision problems, earaches, nightmares, decreased ability to concentrate, blocked intuition, delusion, and the tendency to be overly logical.

The **seventh chakra**, or crown chakra, located at the top of the head, is related to spirituality and higher states of consciousness. Blockages here may cause brain issues, mental illness, difficulties in cognition, depression, confusion, grandiosity, and "spaciness." Someone with a blockage in the seventh chakra may feel ungrounded and spiritually disconnected.

Three more chakras, located at the bottom of the feet, firmly connect you to the core of the planet, send earth energy into your body, and channel out any excess energy. These chakras are used when you need extra grounding.

Four other transpersonal chakras at the top of the head are related to planes of spiritual awareness that exist beyond the crown chakra. Related to cosmic and interstellar consciousness, universal energy, and spiritual realms of mind over matter, they channel this higher awareness to our awakened consciousness.

In addition to the chakras, there are secondary energy centers and connecting subtle energy cords that run down the arms, hands, fingers, legs, feet, toes, and throughout the body. These secondary sources are ultimately connected to the central cord of energy. There are energy centers in the middle of the palms that, when opened, help you to feel subtle energy. These are very important in crystal healing work.

Finally, there are subtle bodies that extend outward from our physical body, each possessing an increasingly fine vibratory rate, and each having to do with a different aspect of our being. The first etheric body surrounding and extending outward from the physical body is the electromagnetic field, or aura. Extending outward from the etheric body are the emotional or astral body, the mental body, and the causal body. Each of these affects our physical body and is, in turn, affected by our physical body. The emotional body and the mental body, both formed from our feelings and thoughts, are the main bodies influenced by crystal healing work.

A very powerful crystal healing method involves training yourself to physically sense or feel the vibration of the extended energy bodies, the subtle energy system, and the chakras to determine what is either blocked or overstimulated. Once you have developed this skill, you can use your crystals to recreate the original balance in the entire subtle energy system, stimulating what needs to be activated or reducing what is overstimulated. When balanced with your crystals and focused intention, the related physical, mental, or emotional illness or disease will tend to clear up. In addition to balancing the entire subtle energy system, you can use your crystals on specific areas that you have determined to be in need of more work. The following chapters will show you exactly how to do this.

Chapter 3

BUILDING YOUR BASIC CRYSTAL HEALING KIT

Having many crystals in your collection does not equate to better healing abilities. As explained in the earlier pages of this book, it is quite possible to be a good crystal healer with just a handful of clear quartz crystals. Strength of focus, the ability to hear your stones, and a broad knowledge of crystal healing techniques are far more important than the number and variety of crystals you have.

Though you can perform all of your crystal healing work using only clear quartz crystals, it is easier to have a basic array of colored crystals so that you won't have to constantly clear and program your clear crystals with different colors. Basically, if you are drawn to a certain type of colored crystal, it is calling to you. No matter the reason, if you wish to add colored crystals as an addition to your clear quartz collection, there are certain ones that are best for healing.

The information provided in the next two chapters will be enough to help you perform all of the amazing healing work you can imagine. I have first provided a list of crystals that are important to include in a basic crystal healing kit. Along with the healing properties of each of these crystals, I have included one or more specific healing techniques that you can use with each of them. Once you have learned these techniques, as well as the ways to use your clear quartz crystals to move energy in the subtle body, there really isn't any type of healing you won't be able to do.

I tend to use the colored stones that correspond to and thereby influence the subtle energy centers and pathways in the physical, mental, emotional, and psychic bodies. I also carry a collection of smaller crystals to link subtle energy pathways so that energy is moved in certain healing patterns. I have a collection of crystals that I call *amplifiers*. These are mostly smaller clear quartz crystals (natural or extremely polished) that I can place on the various colored crystals to amplify the effects of the color.

Because the shade of a color, its degree of opaqueness, and its clarity have effects that subtly alter the effects of both clear and colored crystals, I have an array of opaque, solid, and clear crystals in each color category. You will find these in both the initial and secondary crystal healing kit. Having both clear and opaque colored crystals allows me to fine-tune the work that I do. For instance, if I want to work with the air element, I may use a colored crystal that is more transparent. Similarly, if I want to work with the earth element, I may use an opaque crystal in that color. The degree of opaqueness will determine how much grounding earth element it possesses. Generally speaking, the more transparent the crystal, the more air quality it has, and the more easily it can be used to release or raise energy. The more opaque the crystal, the more grounding it has, and the more I can use it to lower overexcited energy to produce states of calmness.

Even though I list the healing qualities of each crystal in both crystal healing kits, it is important to remember that *the qualities listed for each stone are only strong tendencies and a crystal never does the same thing every time it is used*. This is a vitally important thing to remember when building your healing collection. Nothing in manifested life is static: The stone, the circumstance, you, the environment, and the other person differ every time the crystal is used. Because all of these factors are dynamic, a crystal's general tendencies may subtly change depending on these variations.

The following crystals are essential to include in your first basic crystal healing kit. They include not only an array of the highly versatile clear quartz crystals, but also the colored crystals you will need for every healing eventuality, taking into account color and degree of opacity or clarity. As you begin to work with the stones in this basic collection, you will likely find that other crystals in these categories call to you. They can be added to your secondary healing kit.

THE BASIC CRYSTAL HEALING KIT

The following crystals are essential to include in your basic crystal healing kit. You will be able to do any healing procedure with these crystals.

ONE HAND-SIZED DOUBLE TERMINATED NATURAL CLEAR QUARTZ CRYSTAL AT LEAST 3" IN LENGTH

TWO HAND-SIZED SINGLE TERMINATED NATURAL CLEAR QUARTZ CRYSTALS AT LEAST 3" IN LENGTH

FOUR OR EIGHT SINGLE TERMINATED NATURAL CLEAR QUARTZ CRYSTALS AT LEAST 2½" IN LENGTH

FOUR SINGLE TERMINATED NATURAL CLEAR QUARTZ CRYSTALS ABOUT 1½" IN LENGTH

FOUR OR EIGHT DOUBLE TERMINATED NATURAL CLEAR QUARTZ CRYSTALS ABOUT 1" IN LENGTH

ONE WHITE HOWLITE ABOUT 1½" IN DIAMETER OR LENGTH

ONE SINGLE TERMINATED AMETHYST AT LEAST 3" IN LENGTH AND 1" IN WIDTH

FIVE HAND-SIZED SINGLE TERMINATED AMETHYST CRYSTALS AT LEAST 2" IN LENGTH AND ABOUT ¾" IN WIDTH

EIGHT TUMBLED AMETHYSTS AT LEAST 2" IN WIDTH AND LENGTH

EIGHT AMETHYSTS ABOUT 1" IN LENGTH. ALL EIGHT OF THEM TUMBLED, SINGLE OR DOUBLE TERMINATED

ONE LAPIS LAZULI BETWEEN 1¼" AND 1½" IN LENGTH OR DIAMETER

ONE BLUE SODALITE BETWEEN ½" AND 1" IN DIAMETER

ONE TURQUOISE OR TURQUOISE AMAZONITE BETWEEN ¾" AND 1¼" IN DIAMETER

ONE ROSE QUARTZ AT LEAST 1½" IN DIAMETER OR ABOUT 2" IN LENGTH

ONE RHODOCHROSITE AT LEAST 1½" IN DIAMETER TO BE USED IN PLACE OF ROSE QUARTZ FOR MORE GROUNDING

ONE KELLY GREEN AFRICAN MALACHITE AT LEAST 1½" IN DIAMETER, OR AT LEAST 2" IN LENGTH

TWO LIGHT GREEN CALCITE AT LEAST 1½" TO 2" IN DIAMETER

ONE NATURAL YELLOW CITRINE OR YELLOW JADE ABOUT 1½" IN DIAMETER OR 2" IN LENGTH IF IN A CARVED TERMINATED CRYSTAL SHAPE

ONE ORANGE CARNELIAN ABOUT 1½" IN DIAMETER OR 2" IN LENGTH IN A CARVED TERMINATED CRYSTAL SHAPE

ONE ORANGE-TONED NATURAL AMBER
ABOUT 1½" IN DIAMETER

ONE RED GARNET CRYSTAL AT LEAST 1½"
IN WIDTH AND LENGTH

TWO MEDIUM COLOR SINGLE TERMINATED
NATURAL SMOKY QUARTZ CRYSTALS ABOUT
3" IN LENGTH

ONE BLACK TOURMALINE CRYSTAL AT
LEAST 2" IN LENGTH

These are the basic crystals and stones that you should have in your initial crystal healing kit. The following pages will describe the attributes and uses of each of these stones and give you a specific healing technique that you can use with them. After this explanation, there will be a secondary list of additions that you can make to your first collection of crystals. Of course, if any other crystal is calling to you, you should add it to your assortment. Remember, however, that you can perform any crystal healing with all natural clear quartz crystals or with the initial crystal healing kit listed above.

Chapter 4
BEFORE YOU BEGIN A HEALING SESSION

GET PERMISSION

If you are working to heal someone else, you should always get their permission before you begin; otherwise, the negative energy you release may come back to harm you. This is especially true if they have consciously or unconsciously put up barriers. Permission means that this person is receptive to your healing, and, as a result, it will be more effective. If the person isn't physically present, then you can ask for permission on the etheric planes. Generally speaking, however, try to ask directly before you begin. Of course, there is no problem with sending generic healing energy like love, inner peace, happiness, and good health.

CREATE A SAFE SPACE

Once you have permission to begin, it is vitally important to create a safe space so that the person you are healing feels protected and comfortable. This, too, will help them open up to your healing. You should take care to prevent all possible interruptions, making sure that your children or pets are unable to enter the healing environment. Put your pets where they won't intrude, and make sure your children know to be quiet. You may want to post a sign reminding people not to intrude. Remember to turn your phone off.

It is also important to create a trusting environment before you begin, and to maintain this environment during the healing itself. Be willing to listen completely, without interruption, and with total acceptance. (Accepting is different than condoning.) Make sure that you and the other person are in complete accord. One way to ensure harmony is to mutually open yourselves to each other as you hold hands, look into each other's eyes, and imagine a flow of gentle breath between your hearts.

BE GROUNDED

Be sure that you are well grounded. If you aren't, not only will it be hard to channel the wisdom needed for accurate diagnosis and healing, but you will likely lack the requisite physical, mental, emotional, psychic, and spiritual energy. This is true whether you are healing yourself or someone else. You can use the grounding techniques discussed in earlier chapters.

ERECT A SHIELD

When you are healing someone else, it is important to erect a shield around yourself to prevent drawing in negative energy as you remove it from them. Once you are grounded, close your eyes and use your focused intention to visualize a golden aura of light extending outward a foot or two from your physical body. This will shield not only your physical body, but also your feelings, thoughts, and electromagnetic field. Visualize any unwanted energy deflecting off this shield and entering the earth. Be sure, though, that your shield allows you to remain completely receptive to all that the person you are healing expresses or energetically reveals to you.

CLEAR YOUR CRYSTALS AND STONES

Be sure to clear your crystals and stones of any negative energy or influences that they might have stored in them. Your clear quartz crystals are especially likely to attract and store the energy they are exposed to, so clear them very carefully. You can clear each crystal with breath or intention, but the best way to clear a number of crystals at once is to use the smudging method: Light some sage, sweetgrass, cedar, incense, or other sacred herbs in an abalone shell or a fireproof bowl, then blow or fan the smoke over your crystals until they seem clear. If you are focused as you do this, you will feel a definite sensation once they are clear, and they may even *look* clearer. Be sure to blow or fan the smoke over yourself and the other person so that you are both clear; this will allow energy to flow freely and do its work.

I keep my smudge smoke going during the healing session so that I can clear the other person or myself of any negative energy that might be released as the healing progresses. I run the crystal that I am using through the smoke and then touch its tip or surface to the ground as I visualize negative energy flowing into the earth. When you are finished with the healing, be sure to clear yourself and your stones before you wrap and store them. You can use your smoke and focused intention to clear the other person at the end of the healing. You may also use your focused intention to selectively clear only what you want cleared, leaving any specific healing energy to continue its work after the crystal healing session.

CHARGING AND PROGRAMMING

After you have discerned what it is you intend to heal, you may want to charge or program one or more of your crystals with an influence that will help to empower the healing. For example, you may want to charge your crystals by holding them up to the moon or sun and watching as they absorb lunar or solar energy. Alternatively, you might just visualize moonlight or sunlight entering your crystals. You can charge your stones with any type of energy the healing requires. For example, you may want to counteract a fever by charging your crystal with a gentle, cooling energy; in this case, a clear quartz crystal would work best because clear quartz involves no competing energy of color or stone type. Crystals, especially clear quartz crystals, can be charged or programmed with sound, intention, visualization, other stones, emotion, fire, earth, flowers and plants, ceremony, or any other influence.

HOW TO PROGRAM A CRYSTAL OR STONE

To charge or program a crystal or stone, use both hands to hold it out in front of you at the level of your heart chakra, in the middle of your chest. Then visualize an object, a specific colored stone, a tone, a thought or feeling, or anything you wish, and with one-pointed intention, blow it into your crystal. Keep using your breath to send the chosen influence into your crystal until you get a sense that it is charged. Your crystal will behave however you have programmed it to behave. When you have finished the relevant healing, you may clear the charging or programming from your stone just as you would clear it at any other time.

It is not absolutely necessary to know the locations of the various organs and systems in the body in order to do healing work. If you are sweeping the auric body, you can feel or sense areas that are out of balance whether you know the name of the organ that is represented by a particular energetic anomaly or not. Similarly, you can energetically correct or rebalance these areas and help the underlying organs or biologic systems without being able to name them. However, it is useful to know what these organs and systems are and how they connect so that you can identify where more investigation is needed. If you know, for example, that the heat you feel below the rib cage may represent the kidneys, then you will likely want to work with the kidneys directly. You will likely want to use a crystal or stone, then, to stimulate the kidneys, and because it filters toxins out of the blood and controls the fluid balance and electrolyte levels in the body, you may also want to work with toxicity and the blood.

Chapter 5
SPECIFIC HEALINGS

So far, crystal healing has been explained in this book as a process of creating wholeness from what is broken or out of balance. This is true from a more limited perspective. However, the next step in your growth as a crystal healer is to be able to maintain a larger perspective at the same time, to realize that even though illness is an expression of imbalance, it is also an integral part of a larger whole in which it plays an essential role. In other words, rather than being something "broken off" from what was whole, illness, too, is part of the totality.

To become a more effective healer, it is important to be aware of both realities as you do your crystal work. Also, remain aware that you, too, as a healer are part of this totality. If you perceive the imbalance at the same time as you perceive the larger state of equilibrium, you will then gain the wisdom to make the proper changes for a new, healthier, state of wholeness. In other words, to be most effective, limit your viewpoint in order to "see" the imbalance while at the same time, from a larger perspective, perceive the total and complete wholeness of which the illness is merely an aspect.

In the following pages, each specific method energetically corrects a spiritual, mental, emotional, and physical imbalance through the precise use of crystals and stones. By remaining aware of this essential unity as you employ these crystal and stone healing techniques you will become a deeply effective healer.

IN THE LARGER SENSE,
NOTHING IS REALLY BROKEN
AND NOTHING REALLY CHANGES.
THIS IS THE PARADOX WITHIN WHICH HEALING HAPPENS.

UPPER CHAKRAS

Clear Quartz Crystal

THE WORKHORSE OF ALL CRYSTALS

Clear quartz crystal is the workhorse of the crystal healing because of its power and because it is the most versatile of all the crystals. *There is not one thing that you can do with a colored crystal or stone that you can't also do with clear quartz crystal.* Not only can clear quartz be laid or carried on the body, but you can also use it to actively manipulate energy in the subtle realms in order to affect physical healing. You can use your clear quartz crystal to raise, lower, cut through, remove, and transmit energy. You can use it to vitalize or energize the physical and subtle bodies to help them naturally heal. You can use it to energetically amplify thoughts, feelings, visualizations, and any other manifested form. During a healing, a clear quartz crystal can be used to open or close any subtle energy point in the body and to amplify and empower the effects of any colored stone. You can program it with sound, color, specific intentions, or affirmations in order to influence your body, mind, and feelings accordingly. Quartz crystals can bring you energy, information, and insight to help your healing work. Unlike a colored crystal, clear quartz has no limits other than your own imagination.

White Howlite and Selenite

STRUCTURAL AND ANGELIC CRYSTALS

Associated with white light and combining all color, both white howlite and selenite can be used to help open the upper chakras. Placing these and other white stones above an amethyst on the crown chakra will help stimulate the upper, extended chakras and lead to higher states of consciousness than the open crown chakra alone. (Clear quartz can also be used for this.)

White howlite and selenite are used for immediate calming and can help bring patience, reduce insomnia, and soothe an overactive mental state. White contains an equal balance of all the colors on the spectrum and possesses aspects of each color. As a result, it calms through its qualities of balance, energetic softness, impartiality, and neutrality. White howlite tends to be more grounding than selenite because of its opaqueness. The clearer selenite, related to the angelic realms, connects you to the deep peace and tranquility of those realms.

Because both white howlite and selenite are related to earth energy, they can help strengthen the spine and the core physical structure. Placing these stones on fractured bones can help them knit. Both white howlite and selenite can support the care and healing of muscles and muscular tension, nerves (when combined with citrine), tendons, teeth, fingernails, and toenails. Both stones can be used to slow down bone degeneration because they aid in the absorption of calcium into bones, teeth, and nails. White howlite, more so than selenite, can also help with problematic lactation. Selenite and white howlite may both be used to help heal epilepsy, psoriasis, tumors, and ulcers.

White howlite and selenite can also be used to form a protective aura around the body to absorb any negativity or illness, which can then be cleared away as you clear the stone. Because of its connection with the angels, selenite can be used to form a lighted aura of angelic protection that shields you from negativity, disharmony, or illness. This will be especially effective if you invoke the archangel Michael, or another specific angel, as you do so.

Here is a white howlite crystal healing procedure that you can use to help strengthen the physical skeletal system for yourself or someone else.

STRENGTHENING YOUR BONES WITH WHITE HOWLITE

1. Lie down on your back with your spine straight, head forward, arms beside you, and legs uncrossed. Surround your body with clear quartz crystals. If they have terminations, point the tips inward toward your body. Place one above your head, another below your feet, and the others at your sides—equidistant from each other. Then place a smoky quartz crystal below your feet, tip facing upward, to channel in earth energy.

2. Next, place a white howlite on your abdomen, halfway between your heart chakra and your belly button (navel point). Place two clear quartz crystals above so that they are touching the top of the white howlite and are aligned with the spine, their tips pointing upward toward the head. Next, place two more clear quartz crystals below so that they are touching the bottom of the white howlite and are aligned with the spine, their tips pointing downward toward the feet. You now have a straight line of howlite and quartz overlaying your spine.

3. Next, place a single terminated quartz crystal on each side and touching the white howlite, their tips pointing outward. This forms a cross.

4. Once you have laid the stones, hold your hands, palms upward, in Prithvi Mudra, lightly touching your fourth finger to your thumb with the other three fingers completely extended. They will naturally fan outward. Place a clear quartz crystal, tip pointing upward toward the arm, in the palm of each hand to increase the effects of this hand position.

5. Now, close your eyes. Focus on your breathing, feeling it flow in and out of your nose. Relax on each exhale, releasing any tension your feel anywhere in your body.

6. Once you feel relaxed, visualize that you are surrounded in an aura of white light. Hold this vision for at least one minute, or until you can sense it or clearly visualize it.

7. Now, with every inhale and exhale, imagine that your breath flows into the white howlite and into your spine until your entire spine is filled with it. Once your spine is filled with the white howlite energy, imagine that it flows into every other bone in your body: into the bones of your ribs, your pelvis, your legs and feet, your neck, your arms, your hands and fingers, and then your entire skull. Continue until you visualize every bone as being filled with white howlite energy that glows with pure white light.

8. If you have any fractures, fatigue, or weakness in any of your bones, imagine this white howlite energy knitting together all breaks as it rebuilds and invigorates. If you know of a particular area that needs special attention, imagine sending the howlite white light into that specific area. The earth energy from the smoky quartz will also enter your subtle body to help rebuild its structure.

9. You should do this healing process for thirty minutes a day. If it is difficult to maintain for thirty minutes, you can do it in ten- or twenty-minute segments.

10. When you are finished, slowly open your eyes, then release the hand position and the crystals in your palms. Then remove the other stones in the reverse order in which you placed them.

Prithvi Mudra and white howlite both work to repair and vitalize your physical structure and to channel in the earth element to help heal all of your body's tissues. This healing practice will also work to generally fight disease, build your immunity, relieve ulcers, and improve your overall stamina. It is not recommended, however, to hold Prithvi more than ten minutes if you tend to be depressed, greatly overweight, or have too much of the earth element in your energy field.

Amethyst

THE ENLIGHTENMENT
AND HEALING CRYSTAL

You absolutely must have amethyst in your collection because, other than clear quartz crystal, it is the most versatile crystal for any healing task. *If you don't know what crystal to use in healing, use amethyst.* Amethyst brings physical, mental, and emotional relaxation, while calming stress and anxiety. It channels feminine energy. Associated with the moon, it has gentle and powerful energy that can penetrate any physical, mental, or emotional barrier. It helps counteract fear. It is expansive in nature, so it is good to use for releasing what is cramped or tight within the physical, mental, or emotional body.

Amethyst is the spiritual crystal used for the crown chakra. When placed above or on the top of the head, it can easily connect you with the higher spiritual realms well beyond the physical body, time, and all forms of physical manifestation. Along with the unbounded joy this brings, it can also channel information from higher consciousness to apply to your crystal healing work.

Here is a crystal healing method that you can use with your amethyst crystals. (You can also use clear quartz crystals that have been programmed with amethyst.) This powerful procedure is perhaps the easiest method you can use for a complete healing that will work on all levels. If you don't know what is specifically wrong, or can't quite diagnose the illness, this is a good healing to use.

A BASIC AMETHYST CRYSTAL HEALING FOR ANY AILMENT

1. Lie on your back with your legs uncrossed, spine straight, and your head facing forward. Rest your arms, palms upward, along the sides of your body. Take long, deep, gentle breaths, paying attention to each breath as it enters and leaves through your nostrils. Let your body relax as you do this. If your mind wanders, merely bring it back to your breath. Do this for at least one minute, or until you feel centered, calm, and focused.

2. Surround your body with four, six, or eight amethyst crystals. If your crystals have terminations, point them inward toward your body. Now, close your eyes and visualize that these crystals create an aura of violet light that surrounds your body. Allow a sense of calm peacefulness to enter your mind, body, and emotions. Do this for at least one minute.

3. Next, place an amethyst on your heart chakra in the middle of your chest and imagine that its violet energy enters into and opens this chakra with every inhale. Relax your body and release any negativity with each exhale.

4. Now, place a small amethyst on your third eye (located in the middle of your forehead). As before, draw in the amethyst light with the inhale and relax with the exhale, releasing any negativity.

5. Next, place an amethyst on your third chakra (located about two inches above your navel). Draw in amethyst light with the inhale, relaxing and releasing with the exhale.

6. Now place another small amethyst on your throat chakra (located midway down your neck). Feel its energy entering your throat chakra with each inhale, while releasing negativity with each exhale.

7. Next, place an amethyst on your second chakra (located about two inches below your navel point, or belly button). As before, draw the amethyst light into this chakra while you inhale, releasing negativity with your exhale.

8. Now, place an amethyst, tip pointing downward if its terminated, on your first chakra (located near the base of your spine). As before, draw amethyst light into this chakra while relaxing and releasing negative energy.

9. Next, place an amethyst, tip pointing downward if it is single terminated, above the crown of your head. Visualize drawing violet energy into the crown with every inhale. With every exhale, relax and release all negativity.

10. Finally, place either an amethyst or clear quartz crystal in each hand, tips pointing up toward the arms. With your eyes closed, visualize the crystals continuing to send their violet energy inside you, healing anything that needs healing (whether you consciously know of it or not). Relax your body. If your mind wanders, just bring your attention back to this process. If you have a particular healing task in mind, silently direct the amethysts to that task. Continue this for at least twenty minutes.

When you are finished, open your eyes and carefully remove the crystals in the reverse order in which you placed them.

Royal Blue Lapis Lazuli and Sodalite

THE PSYCHIC CRYSTALS

These royal blue stones are used on the third eye chakra in the middle of the forehead to help increase mental abilities and intuitive powers and to develop psychic, clairaudient, and clairvoyant abilities—enabling you to sense realities well beyond the physical and intellectual. Lapis possesses a more uplifting quality, whereas blue sodalite is more grounding. Together, they can help maintain balance as this upper chakra opens.

Opening the third eye accesses intuitive and psychic powers. This will help you discover areas that need healing, identify causes of damage, and select appropriate healing methods. Intellectualizing will often limit you to working on a more superficial level.

The following healing practice will help open the third eye chakra, increasing your sensitivity to subtle energy and to your crystals. It can be performed on yourself and on others.

OPENING THE THIRD EYE WITH LAPIS LAZULI AND CLEAR CRYSTAL

1. Lie down on your back with your spine straight, head forward, and legs uncrossed.

2. Surround your body with four, six, or eight single terminated, clear quartz crystals, their points facing toward your body. This will create an empowering aura. Place one crystal above your head, another below your feet, and the rest equidistant from each other on both sides of your body.

3. Place an orange crystal on your belly about two inches below your navel point (belly button). This will help balance the energy of the third eye as it opens, providing grounding, empowerment, and the ability to manifest what you envision.

4. Now, place a lapis lazuli or blue sodalite on your third eye (in the middle of your forehead) with the tip upward if it is terminated.

5. Hold both hands alongside your body, palms upward, in Buddhi Mudra, lightly touching your fifth fingers to your thumbs. (This mudra increases your psychic and intuitive powers.) Place either a lapis lazuli or blue sodalite in each hand as you maintain this mudra.

6. Now, close your eyes. Shift your focus to your breath, breathing with long, deep, gentle breaths while feeling the breath pass in and out of your nostrils. Relax on every exhale. If your mind wanders, bring it back to your breath. Continue until you feel completely calm and focused.

7. Next, visualize that the ring of clear quartz crystals surrounding you glows with increasing brightness to form a radiant ring of protective and vitalizing white light.

8. Now, imagine that with every inhale, each glowing quartz crystal sends a radiant beam of powerful, clear light into the lapis lazuli or blue sodalite on your forehead, amplifying its energy. Relax on the exhale. Do this for three minutes.

9. Next, while focusing on your third eye, imagine that with every inhale, the deep, royal-blue energy of the sodalite or lapis in the center of your forehead flows into your third eye as you repeat the sound om (ohm) silently or out loud. Release any tension or tightness in your forehead with every exhale. Do this for at least three minutes at first. Then, increase your time.

10. When you are finished, sit silently within the awareness created by this practice. Then, imagine that the white light aura slowly draws into your body. When you are ready, open your eyes and remove the crystals in the reverse order in which you placed them.

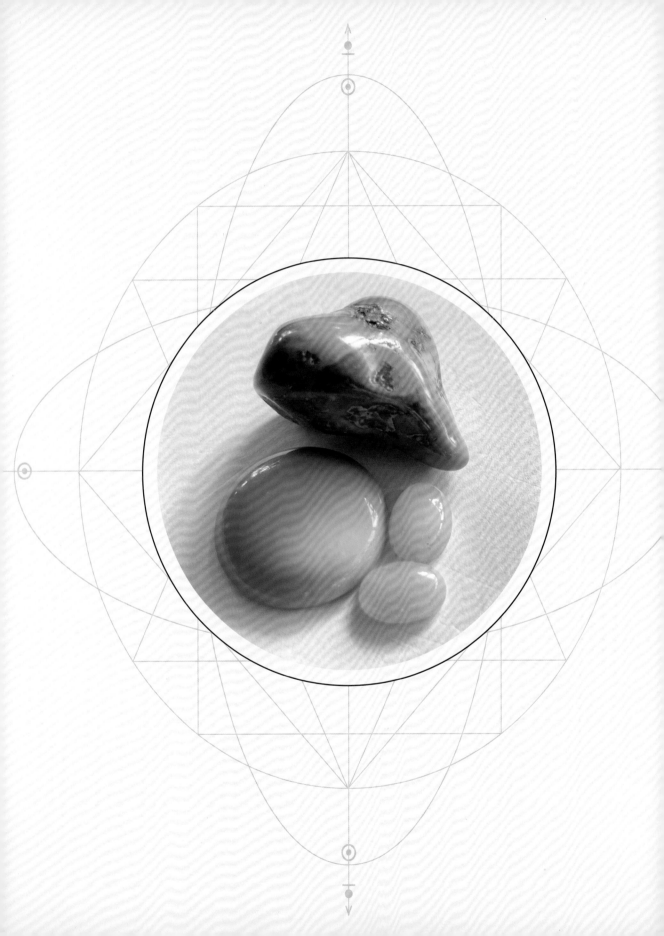

Turquoise or Amazonite

THE COMMUNICATION CRYSTALS

Turquoise or amazonite crystals or stones are used on the throat chakra to open up your ability to communicate with others, to release any communications that you have withheld and suppressed, to help you find the words to express yourself, or to communicate the deepest truths of your soul. Anytime you have refused to express yourself out of fear, embarrassment, shame, or any other such emotion, these unexpressed thoughts or communications lodge themselves in and block the throat chakra.

A blocked throat chakra is often an underlying cause of illnesses or issues with the throat, neck, ears, jaw, mouth, lungs, and bronchial tubes. It can manifest as sore throats or laryngitis, breathing difficulties, recurring cough, swollen glands and neck, or even as more complicated issues like throat cancer. Though these issues may have well-documented physical causes, clearing blockages and activating the throat chakra may contribute to the healing of the physical causes and the illness itself.

The throat chakra also helps regulate the thyroid gland, so if it is blocked it may lead to hypothyroidism, low hormone production, weight gain, excessive fatigue, and muscular weakness. Similarly, if it is overstimulated, it can lead to hyperthyroidism, accelerating your body's metabolism and leading to excessive and uncontrollable weight loss, digestive problems, and rapid heartbeat, among other symptoms.

Not only does turquoise or amazonite help open the throat chakra, but it is also a good stone to use any time you need to release something that is stuck in the body, mind, or emotions. It is known to soak up or remove all forms of negativity from the body or mind, channeling those energies into itself. After the turquoise or amazonite has done this, you merely clear it of the negativity, usually sending it into the earth or smudging it.

Here is a healing practice that you can perform on others or on yourself in order to open or stimulate the throat chakra with turquoise and quartz crystals.

OPENING THE THROAT CHAKRA WITH TURQUOISE AND CLEAR CRYSTAL

1. Lie down on your back with your legs uncrossed, your spine straight, and your head facing forward. Relax your body, centering your mind upon your breath until you are completely focused.

2. Surround your body with four, six, or eight clear quartz crystals pointing inward toward the body. Place one above the head, another below the feet, and the rest equidistant from each other at the sides of your body. Visualize that they surround you in an aura of empowering, energizing light.

3. Next, place a turquoise on your throat chakra (located midway down your neck). Hold your hands in Granthita or Knot Mudra on your navel point. To do this, interlace the fifth, fourth, and third fingers. Touch your second fingers to your thumbs while forming an interlocking circle. To increase the effects of this hand position, hold a double terminated clear quartz crystal between the two palms, or a single terminated crystal with the point facing toward your arms.

4. Next, imagine that the energy from all of the crystals surrounding you sends a beam of clear light into the turquoise on your throat, amplifying its energy. Do this for at least a minute.

5. Now, as you inhale, visualize the energy of the charged turquoise entering, opening, and activating your throat chakra as you silently repeat the sound *ham* (*hahm*). Relax and release any negativity with every exhale. Continue this for at least twenty minutes.

6. When you are finished, imagine that the clear crystal aura completely enters your body. Then, open your eyes and remove the quartz crystals and turquoise in the reverse order in which you placed them.

HEART CHAKRAS

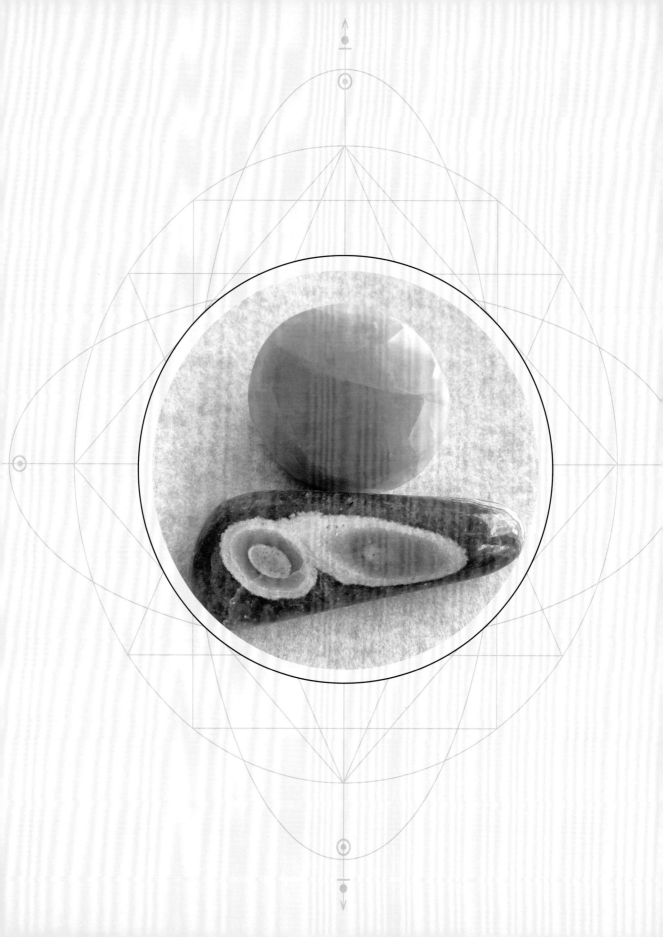

Rose Quartz or Rhodochrosite

THE LOVE CRYSTALS

The heart chakra, located in the middle of your chest, forms a bridge between the lower three chakras of the physical realm and the upper three chakras of the spiritual world. When open, it will help integrate the two in a blending of earth and sky. With this openness and integration, you become fearless, confident, loving, compassionate, empathetic, and kind; your everyday world becomes spiritualized, and you experience everything in physical manifestation as an expression of the divine.

Though the traditional yogic color associated with the heart chakra is green, all pink crystals, minerals, or stones also help open the heart chakra. So, too, do energetically sky-like, opaque, or even totally clear rose. Rhodochrosite, which possesses a denser color, can be used to open the heart chakra if you need more grounding than rose quartz provides.

Rose quartz is another essential crystal to have in your main healing kit. In addition to opening the heart center, rose quartz can be used any time you need to add a gentle, soothing quality to your healing. For example, if someone is suffering from PTSD, rose quartz will help to calm distressing memories. It is a crystal that tends to help open emotions and parts of the physical body, and it brings a level of self-acceptance that makes someone feel safe to let go. When you need to bring warmth to what is cold and detached but don't want the intense fire qualities of the red, yellow, or orange stones, then rose quartz, rhodochrosite, or other pink crystals are good to use.

It is important to open the heart chakra for its empathetic and loving qualities and because the heart—just like the mind, the third eye, and the crown chakra—is a source of wisdom. Each source sees from a different perspective; the third eye sees beyond the thoughts of the brain, and the open heart sees from the perspective of love and the deeper self within. The blending of the two brings a more complete wisdom. The energetic heart center is the gateway to the experience of the true self; it allows you to become one with the divine, the center of your own being, and the being of the universe. Any time that you perform your crystal healing, then, it is vital that you refer to the wisdom gained from both the heart and the third eye.

Rose quartz may be the most important crystal to use when working with emotional healing. It helps bring unacknowledged or repressed feelings to the surface, and it helps access deeper feelings. It can relieve feelings of shame while bringing self-acceptance, acceptance of others, and acceptance of your life circumstances. Rose quartz and rhodochrosite will help counteract hatefulness, disdain, despair, feelings of being unloved or unloving, and any other emotional states that lead to disharmony and illness.

Because an open heart provides balance for the entire being, it is good to start and end every crystal healing session by placing a rose quartz, a clear quartz crystal, or another pink stone on the heart chakra, ensuring that this chakra remains stimulated and open.

You should include at least one rose quartz that sits comfortably on the heart center in your initial healing stone collection. Because rose quartz is so important when working with emotional healing, it is good to have an extra four or six at hand; this will allow you to place them around the body, thus creating a surrounding, loving aura. You can use either chunks of rose quartz, or tumbled stones that are a couple of inches in diameter. Or, if your goal is to direct energy, you can use four roughly 2.5-inch rose quartz crystals with carved terminations.

The following is a simple and effective crystal healing practice meant to stimulate and open the vitally important energy center of the heart.

ROSE QUARTZ PRACTICE TO HEAL THE WOUNDED HEART

1. Lie down on your back, on a comfortable surface, with your legs uncrossed and your spine straight. You can also sit upright with your spine straight and head facing forward. Place four clear quartz crystals around your body with their tips pointing inward to amplify the effects of this procedure. If you are lying down, place a clear quartz above your head, another below your feet, and one at each side of your body. If you are sitting upright, place the first clear quartz directly in front of you, the other behind you, and one at each of your sides.

2. Next, place a rose quartz crystal on your heart chakra in the center of your chest. If it is terminated, point the tip toward your head. If you are sitting, wear a rose quartz pendant that is long enough for it to rest over your heart chakra.

3. Place the palm of your right hand on top of the rose quartz and your heart center, as if you are blessing yourself. Place your left hand on top of your left leg with your palm facing upward in receptive position. Place another rose quartz or clear quartz crystal in the center of your left hand. If the stone is terminated, point its tip toward your arm.

4. Now, with your eyes closed, begin to take gentle, deep breaths. As you inhale, imagine that your breath flows in through your receptive left hand to enter and charge your heart center. Relax on your exhale, letting go of all tension. Do this for at least three minutes.

5. Next, imagine that with each breath, a gently glowing pink light flows into your entire body to fill it with loving, accepting, compassionate energy. Then imagine that it spills out from your body to surround you in a gentle pink aura. Relax and silently repeat these sentences, one with each breath: "I am loving"; "I am loved"; "I am love." Do this for at least three minutes and up to twenty minutes.

6. When you are finished, bring your attention back to your breath. With each inhale, imagine gathering all of the loving pink light and energy deeply into the heart of your soul.

7. When you are ready, open your eyes and remove the crystals in the reverse order in which you placed them.

A WOUNDED HEART IS OFTEN AT THE HEART OF ILLNESS; HEAL THE HEART TO HEAL THE ILLNESS.

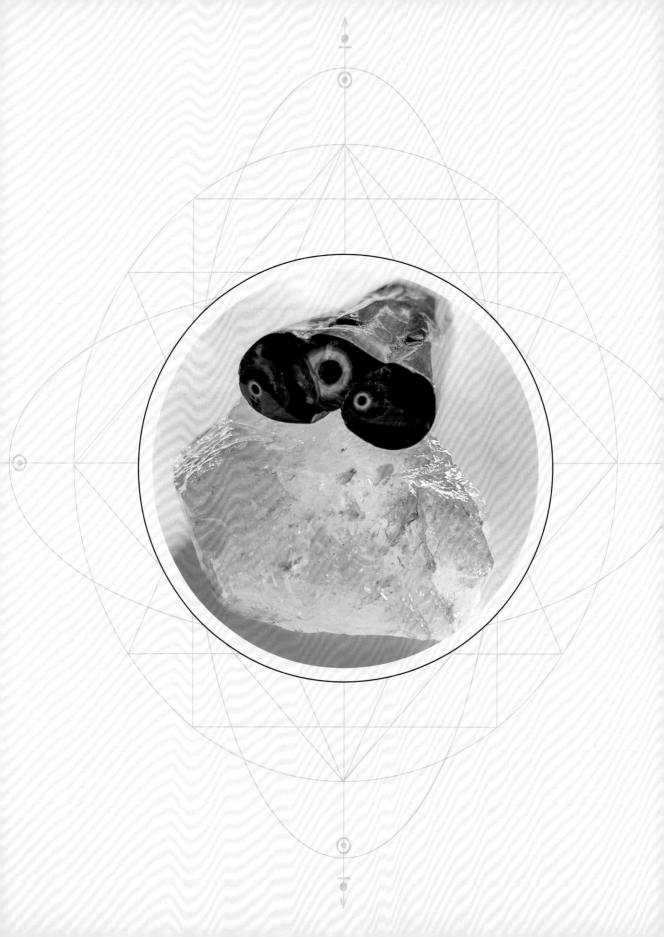

Green Calcite
or Malachite
THE NURTURING HEART STONES

All green crystals or stones will work to open the heart chakra. Green crystals or stones often tend to work more on the physical aspects of the heart, whereas rose quartz or the pink crystals and stones tend to work more on the emotional aspects of the heart. Because there are no hard-and-fast rules, however, you will need to tune into the heart, the heart chakra, and the stones themselves to see which ones you want to use.

Green malachite or green calcites are excellent crystals to use to counteract and heal fever, infection, inflammation, pain, anger, anxiety, and anything else that is fire-like in its nature. They will help soothe injuries like broken bones, sprains, body spasms, or deep cuts. Place these stones on the injury and use your clear quartz crystal to draw out pain and other reactions. If you need more grounding when working with green crystals, use malachite. If you need more gentle soothing, use green calcite.

All green crystals, including malachite and green calcite, can be used to bring a sense of prosperity and to attract wealth, especially if combined with visualization. They also channel in the restorative and nurturing energy of nature, nature devas, and the earth. These nature spirits and devas have a special affinity with crystal and, when called upon, can guide your crystal healing.

Use malachite or green calcite when healing any physical illness or disease of the heart. You can directly apply them to the heart chakra or place them above the physical heart location as you visualize their energy entering into the heart muscle and the surrounding veins and arteries. You can add garnets or other red crystals to your work with the physical heart, tracing their trajectories as you scan for blockages or other impediments. Adding amethyst will increase the healing effect.

With any issue of the physical heart, there are other contributing mental, emotional, and physical factors. It is a good idea, then, to use your other crystals to address these issues while working to heal the physical heart. If the person lives in a state of constant rage and hypertension, for example, and eats primarily red meat and sugar, you can use your crystals to calm the rage and hypertension, help manifest dietary changes with crystal visualizations, and also work to heal the heart.

Here is a crystal healing practice using green malachite to work directly on the physical heart. It can be performed on yourself or on others.

MALACHITE
HEART HEALING PRACTICE

1. Sit upright with your spine straight and your feet flat on the ground.

2. Surround yourself with clear quartz crystals, pointing their tips inward toward the body. You can use four, six, or eight, placing one in front of you, another behind you, and the others beside you with equal distance between them. These crystals will help you concentrate and amplify the effects of the green malachite.

3. Next, place a green malachite crystal on your heart chakra (located in the middle of your chest). You can do so by wearing a malachite necklace with the stone resting right upon your heart center. Close your eyes and focus on your breath. With every inhale, imagine that the malachite energy—in the form of green light—enters into and fills your heart center and then your entire body. Relax any tension in your body with every exhale. Do this for at least three minutes.

4. Now, hold your hands in the heart-opening Ganesha Mudra, or Bear Grip, at the level of your chest. To do this, hold your left palm facing outward while facing the palm of the right hand toward it. Now, clasp the fingers of the left hand with the fingers of the right hand, the curled fingers forming a fist.

5. Next, inhale and then deeply exhale while stretching both hands away from each other without pulling them apart. Keep them at chest level. Then, take a slow, deep inhale as you release the stretch. Do this slowly six times. Silently repeat the sound *yam* (*yahm*) with every exhale.

6. After six times slowly exhaling and inhaling while alternatively stretching and releasing the hands, reverse the direction of the hands, facing your right hand outwards from your chest with your left hand on top. Again, without releasing your grip, stretch the hands against each other as you exhale and silently repeat *yam*, releasing the stretch on your inhale. Do this six times.

7. You should perform this sequence at least six times with each hand position. If you have the strength and desire, you can do six more sequences in each hand position. Continue to repeat in sets of twelve (six on each side) for as long as you like.

8. When you are finished, open your eyes and consciously remove the crystals in the reverse order in which you placed them.

This healing practice is especially good for strengthening your physical heart and opening your heart chakra. It can help with all causes of heart disease and heart attack, and it can aid recovery. You can add amethyst to this healing practice by alternating four amethysts with the four clear quartz crystals that surround the body.

LOWER CHAKRAS

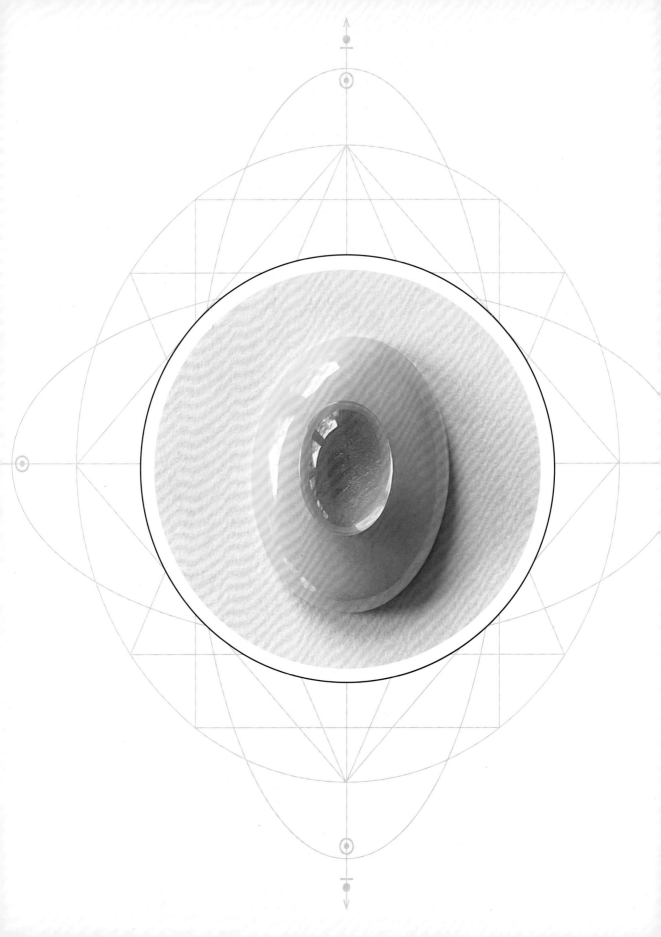

Yellow Citrine or Yellow Jade

THE ENERGY CRYSTALS

All yellow crystals and stones help boost the subtle and physical nervous systems. Clear stones like yellow citrine, yellow topaz, and yellow calcite will add the element of air and tend to be uplifting. The more opaque stones such as yellow jade and yellow tiger eye have more of the earth element in them and tend to be grounding. When the nervous system is stressed, it is good to provide it both energy and calm. If you only have clear yellow crystals, you can couple them with smoky quartz or another grounding stone to provide the needed calm.

Yellow citrine is a very powerful stone for use on the third chakra (the energy center that is about two inches above the navel point, or belly button). It will increase the male solar energy within the subtle bodies, decrease depression, and instill a sense of joy. It will bring warmth to any part of the subtle or physical bodies that feel cold or frozen, including thoughts and feelings. An imbalanced or weak third chakra will tend to make you feel either timid and easily frightened or the opposite: overly dominating and angry. Passive aggressiveness, a lack of self-worth, or hidden shame may be issues related to a weak or imbalanced navel energy center.

It is vitally important to energize the third chakra, or navel point, so that the life force can properly flow through the body. The navel point is where 72,000 subtle nerves converge to then carry the life force through thousands of subtle nerve channels. It is also an important center of energy transformation within the body; it is the site where subtle energetic currents are adjusted in ratio and intensity. As such, it is essential that this center be revitalized if it is depleted by stress, anger, poor diet, or other such contributory factors.

Generally speaking, without a properly functioning third chakra, it is very difficult to raise the subtle energy into the higher chakras, which bring a higher level of consciousness. To help with this, you can place a yellow citrine on the third chakra while also using turquoise, blue lapis, amethyst, or other similarly colored crystals on the throat, third eye, and crown chakras.

Here is a crystal practice with yellow citrine that will help energize the subtle nervous system and the third chakra. Try doing it as a thirty-day practice. If you need more grounding, use yellow jade.

YELLOW CITRINE FOR A STRONG NERVOUS SYSTEM

1. Lie down on your back on a comfortable surface, your head facing forward, your arms down by the sides of your body, palms upward, and your legs uncrossed.

2. Place a single terminated clear quartz crystal with its tip pointing upward above your head. Place a smoky quartz below your feet with the tip pointing downward. Place another single terminated clear quartz on each side of the body, parallel to each other, so that the body is surrounded by a protective and balanced aura.

3. Focus on your breathing. Imagine that your inhale increases the strength of the crystal aura. With every exhale, relax your belly. Do this for at least eleven long, deep breaths, or until the belly is completely relaxed.

4. Next, place a single terminated yellow citrine on the belly button. Point its tip upward so the subtle energy that is released will flow into the upper chakras. Place four clear quartz crystals, tips pointing inward, around the citrine crystal: one above, another below, and the other two on each side—parallel to the citrine.

5. Now, hold your hands in Rudra Mudra with the second and ring fingers touching the thumb and with the third and fifth fingers extended. This mudra will help strengthen the third chakra and help build self-confidence, personal power, and a sense of capability. To amplify the mudra, place a single terminated clear quartz crystal in the middle of the hands as they maintain this position. Inhale strength and energy. Relax with the exhale, silently saying the sound *ram* (*rahm*). Continue this for at least three minutes.

When finished, rest with your eyes closed for a few moments, letting the effects circulate through the subtle nervous system. Then, with eyes open, release the hand position. Remove all of the crystals in the opposite order in which they were placed.

Orange Carnelian and Amber

MANIFESTING CRYSTALS

All orange crystals and stones help stimulate or open the second chakra, the energy center that is located about two to three inches below the belly button and in the sexual organs. Related to water, the second chakra bridges, processes, and integrates the earth energies received through the first chakra and the emotional energies of the subtle nervous system. Orange in color, this energy center is home to passion, romance, creativity, and intimacy. If closed or undeveloped, a person may confuse sex with love and have stunted emotional boundaries and a need to control others. The second chakra is related to the kidneys, adrenals, urinary tract, intestines, and lower back. It is associated with power, money, and sex. It is the center of manifestation and creativity.

Orange carnelian, a member of the quartz family, is an excellent crystal for the second chakra. Along with increasing fertility and sexual potency, its empowerment brings confidence, creativity, motivation, endurance, passion, courage, and the ability to manifest anything in your life.

Orange-toned amber can also help access creativity and the ability to manifest. Related to the sun, its solar energies are gently warming, as compared to carnelian's more intense fire. It allows second chakra work to proceed with less confrontation and fear. Known as a woman's stone, it is used to help with all female-oriented physical problems. It can be used during childbirth, either held in the hands during the birth or worn on the body. Like turquoise, it is also known to absorb and transmute negativity.

Here is a crystal practice that will help stimulate and heal any issues with your adrenals, kidneys, and urinary tract. It will give you the strength and endurance that you need to manifest what you desire. It will also help stimulate your erotic sensuality and help you resolve sexual issues.

ORANGE CARNELIAN PRACTICE FOR ADRENAL, KIDNEY, URINARY TRACT, AND SEXUAL HEALING

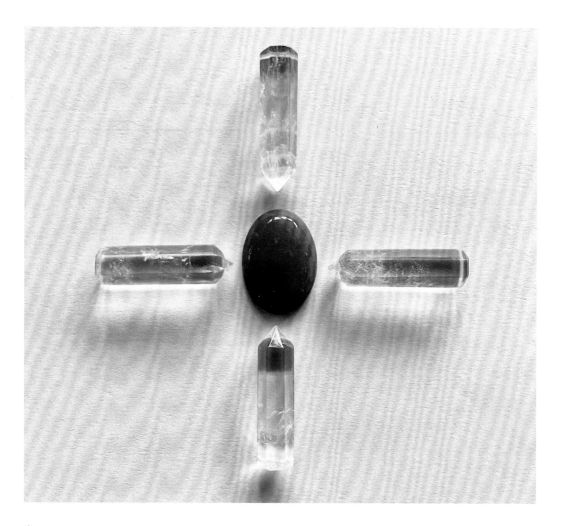

1. Find a comfortable surface and lie down on your back with your head forward, your legs uncrossed, your arms alongside your body, and your palms facing upward.

2. Surround your body with four single terminated clear quartz crystals with their tips pointing in toward your body. Place one above your head, another below your feet, and one on each side of your body—parallel with each other. If you like, you can use eight clear quartz single terminated crystals, placing one equidistant and between the other crystals so that you have three crystals on each side of your body.

3. With your eyes closed, visualize that the clear crystals are connected to a line of energy that surrounds you with an amplifying and protective aura of clear light. With every inhale, imagine that you breathe this protective and energizing light into your body. Relax your body on every exhale. Do this until you feel completely relaxed.

4. Now, open your eyes and place a carnelian crystal on your belly, just above your pubic bone. If the crystal is terminated, point the tip downward to link you to the earth energies. Now, place four amplifying clear quartz crystals around the carnelian: one above, another below, and one on each side.

5. Next, hold a carnelian, an orange citrine, or a clear quartz crystal in each upward-facing palm. If the crystal is terminated, point the tip upward toward your arms to help channel energy into your body. Closing your eyes, visualize a line of connection from the crystals in your hands to the orange carnelian on your belly.

6. Now, focus on your breathing, visualizing that it flows in and out of the carnelian and your second chakra. Imagine that every inhale charges and amplifies the energy of the carnelian. With every exhale, relax your pelvis and the small of your back as you imagine all negativity flowing down from your pelvis and into the earth. Do this for eleven long, deep, relaxed inhales and exhales.

7. Next, imagine a whirling disc of orange light in your second chakra, beneath the carnelian. With every inhale, visualize that this vibrant disc expands and whirls faster and faster. With every exhale, silently repeat the sound *vam* (*vahm*), the sacred sound of the second chakra. Continue for at least seven minutes, or until your entire belly, pelvis, and lower back are filled with vibrant orange light. Feel the light feeding your adrenals, kidneys, urinary tract, and sexual organs with vibrant, healing energy. Continue to relax your pelvis, belly, and lower back as you do this.

8. Once you are finished, imagine that the orange light expands to flow throughout your entire body. As your body fills with this powerful orange light, repeat these words to yourself: "I am confident, creative, and powerful." Do this for at least three minutes, and then silently rest within the energy of this powerful crystal practice.

9. When you are ready, open your eyes and gently remove the crystals in the opposite order in which you placed them.

10. If you are a woman and want to work with reproductive or any other female healing issues, you can do this same practice with amber in place of carnelian. Every place where you used carnelian, just replace it with amber. Instead of imagining a whirling orange disc, visualize a radiant circle of amber light that glows more and more brightly to then expand throughout your body. You can still silently repeat the sound *vam* (*vahm*). Instead of the affirmations used with the carnelian, however, silently repeat these words to yourself: "The universal mother shines within me. i am sensual, creative, and abundant."

Red Garnet or Red Jasper

THE SECURITY CRYSTALS

All red crystals, related to the earth element, can be used to open or stimulate the first (root) chakra, located near the last three vertebrae and the base of your spine. Governing your inner sense of security, an energized first chakra instills confidence that you can survive and thrive in the world. It brings vitality and strength as it roots you solidly into your earthly manifestation; it strengthens your resistance to illness and your immunity to disease. Related to your basic instincts, the first chakra is also connected to sexuality—but more in terms of the satisfaction of a basic need than as a means of relationship and intimacy (which is linked to the second chakra). Just as the energy flow of the crown chakra moves upward to connect with the heavenly realms, the energy flow from the first chakra extends downward into the earth.

Red garnet is an excellent crystal to open and balance the first chakra. Applying it to the base of the spine will help open any blockages that keep you from feeling secure and safe. If your energies are scattered, or if you feel exhausted, excessively negative, greedy, paranoid, or overwhelmed by any other fear-based symptom, you can use red garnet to vitalize your energy center and transmute those feelings.

If garnet is too stimulating, you can substitute red jasper. Red jasper combines the fire of the garnet with more of the earth element, calming the excitability of an opened first chakra.

Red garnet will also help with any disorders of the blood or the circulatory system. To address such problems, place the red garnet where there are blockages in the arteries or veins, rather than placing it on or near the first chakra. Red garnet can also be applied to the heart when there are issues involving blood flow through the chambers of the heart. If the blood flow isn't reaching certain places in the body, applying red garnet to the area lacking blood can help restore flow. Of course, any work involving the heart and blood disorders should be performed in conjunction with a medical professional.

Illnesses that manifest as cold or dull can be heated and healed by using red garnet, ruby, or any other red crystal or stone. As you scan the body, you will be able to feel chilly areas of imbalance and depleted life force. Place red garnet or another red crystal in those places, until you feel a sense of warmth return. Sluggish organs, depression, detachment, and hopelessness also benefit from the application of garnet, ruby, or another red stone.

Red garnet or ruby helps heal the male reproductive system and general male potency. It also helps the bladder, coccyx, legs, knees, feet, and spine—especially the bottom three vertebrae. It can balance negative energies or diseases involving the muscles, veins, nerves, and arteries of the perineum. It also helps stimulate that area.

RED GARNET HEALING FOR VITALITY AND PERSONAL POWER

1. Lie on your back with your head forward, your arms down by your sides, your palms upward, and your legs uncrossed.

2. Program four or eight single terminated clear quartz crystals with the color red. Place them around your body at a distance of about six inches to create a strengthening aura. Pointing the crystal tips inward, place one stone above your head and another below your feet. Place the others by your sides, parallel with and equidistant to each other, with their tips also facing inward. Imagine that these crystals are connected to form an energizing aura of red light around your body.

3. Next, place a red garnet between your legs at the base of your spine, tip downward if it is terminated. Then, in order to balance the stimulation of your first chakra, place a light green calcite on your heart chakra.

4. Now, hold your hands in Gyan Mudra, with your pointer fingers touching the tips of your thumbs and with the other fingers extended. This hand position will help bring calmness, receptivity, and stability as you open to the powerful effects of this healing. Place a single terminated clear quartz crystal in each palm as you hold this mudra. Point the tips of the crystals toward your arms.

5. Now, close your eyes and focus on your breathing. Imagine that every inhale flows into the green calcite and your heart chakra, softening your chest. With every exhale, relax the small of your back, your buttocks, pelvis, belly, and any place that feels tense. Imagine the breath flowing down your body, out your feet, and into the earth. Do this for three minutes, or until you feel relaxed.

6. Next, shift your focus to the red garnet near the base of your spine. With every inhale, imagine that its energy flows into your first chakra, causing it to glow with a brilliant red light. With every exhale, visualize that this brilliant red glow flows downward as a red stream of light to form a strong root, anchoring you deeply into the earth. This earth energy will bring you a strong sense of personal power, security, safety, and effectiveness. Do this for at least seven minutes or up to an hour.

7. When you are finished, release the Gyan Mudra hand position and put the crystals down beside you. With your eyes closed, place both hands, palms down, right hand on top of the left hand, upon the green calcite and your heart chakra. Imagine that your breathing now flows in and out of your heart chakra. Silently repeat these words to yourself: "I am loving, safe, and powerful." Continue doing this for at least three minutes.

8. When you feel ready, open your eyes and remove all of the crystals in the reverse order in which you placed them.

When doing this healing practice, be sure that your heart chakra and root chakra are equally open so that you do not overstimulate your root chakra. The heart chakra links and balances all of the upper and lower energy centers. We must be sure to strengthen and vitalize the heart chakra whenever we open the third eye and the crown chakra, access the power and lust of the second and third chakras, or activate the root chakra. That is why we use green calcite in conjunction with red garnet in this crystal healing practice.

LOVE MUST ALWAYS BALANCE POWER.

GROUNDING CRYSTALS

Smoky Quartz

THE ENERGY CRYSTALS

Smoky quartz is a wonderful crystal to use for grounding your energy into the earth, which is absolutely necessary if you are going to perform any type of healing work. The more that you plant your energetic roots into the earth, the more you can draw on their strength to access the higher energy centers. Being able to access the intuitive and psychic third eye center and the expanded awareness of the crown chakra will give you the information needed to diagnose and treat physical, mental, and emotional disease and imbalance. Grounding provides a balance for your heart chakra so that you have the ability to keep it open enough to hear its wisdom, especially with respect to emotional healing.

Grounding not only helps you access the awareness of the higher energy centers but also vitalizes your entire subtle body with the powerful energy of the earth. It will provide balancing calmness when you stimulate the third chakra to work with the subtle and physical nervous systems.

Smoky quartz is useful anytime that you are working with physical, emotional, or mental tension. It helps to alleviate stress, anxiety, hyperactivity, overstimulation of any chakra, and agitation caused by any illness or physical condition. It can be combined with rose quartz and/ or amethyst for healings that require soothing energy.

Smoky quartz, and all brown stones, are related to the minor chakras that help balance and assimilate the magnetic life force currents of the earth. Those chakras are located in the center of the arch of each foot. Brown stones are energy transformers, regulating the intensity and quantity of the life-force energy that enters from the earth, as well as the excess energy discharged by the body into the earth. This constant flow of connection provides a sense of stability and safety. It helps you harmonize with the rhythms of the natural world. Psychologically, it maintains your link to the immediate earth-plane reality, providing a secure and healthy foundation for the entire subtle and physical bodies. Stimulating the energy chakras in the feet will also repair issues with the feet, ankles, and legs.

Just as amethyst and other colored forms of quartz result from natural processes and mineral inclusions over millennia, smoky quartz is created when clear quartz is naturally irradiated deep within the earth for millions of years. There are several types of smoky quartz, ranging from very pale brown to those that are so dark as to appear opaque black. Morion, a German, Danish, Spanish, and Polish synonym for smoky quartz, tends to manifest this darker shade. Cairngorm stone, which is found in the Scottish Cairngorm Mountains, can range from yellow-brown to pure smoky brown to grayish brown. No matter what variation of smoky quartz you use, the darker it is, the more deeply it will ground you.

When grounding is needed, you can place smoky quartz by or between the feet if you are sitting or standing, or below the feet if you are lying on your back. If the stone is single terminated, point the tip away from the feet and visualize the energy from it connecting deeply into the earth. If you want to bring earth energy into the body, point the tip toward the body. If you only want to add some gentle grounding when doing healing work, use a lighter color of smoky quartz. If you want deeper grounding, use a darker color.

You can place smoky quartz directly upon any area of the body that needs soothing. To calm mental issues, place the smoky quartz—along with lapis or another blue crystal—on the forehead. Point the tip downward. To relieve persistently troubling emotions, place the smoky quartz, tip downward, on the heart center, along with a pink or light green crystal.

Here is a smoky quartz healing procedure that you can use when immediate and deep grounding is needed for extreme cases of anxiety, as well as physical, mental, or emotional agitation.

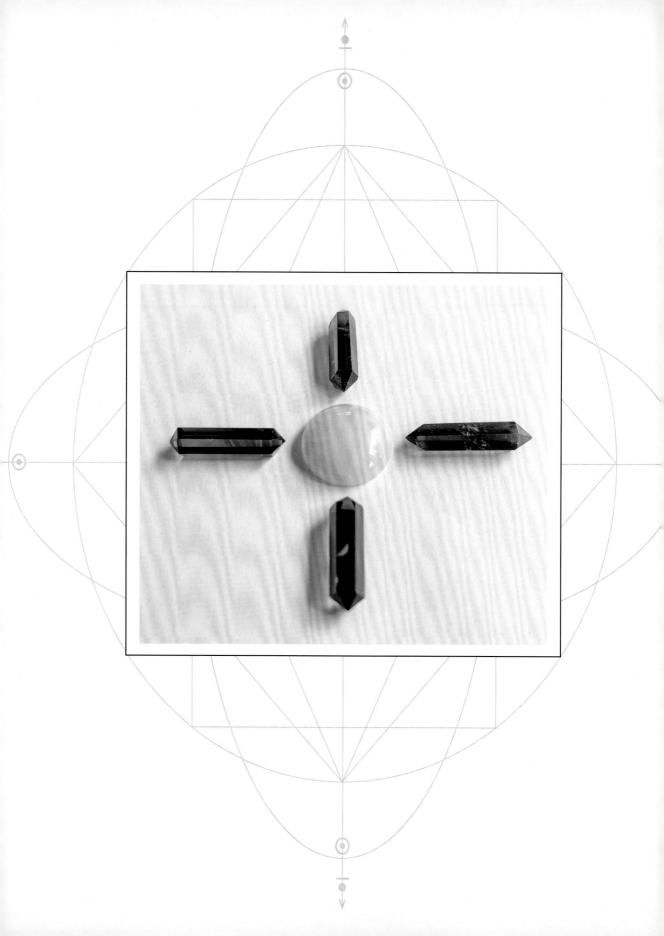

SMOKY QUARTZ
DEEP RELAXATION PRACTICE

1. Lie on your back with your spine straight and legs uncrossed, or sit upright in a straight-backed chair in lotus or half-lotus position. Place your feet side by side, flat upon the ground, if you are sitting. Surround your body with four or eight clear quartz crystals that you have programmed to be a medium smoky brown color. Point the tips outward to channel away tension or any other negativity that is released during this crystal healing procedure. Imagine that a line of earth-colored light connects each of the crystals surrounding you in a protective and soothing aura.

2. If you are lying on your back, place a smoky quartz crystal below your feet with the tip pointing downward. If you have two smoky quartz crystals, use one below the center of each foot. If sitting up, lay the smoky quartz between your feet with the tip pointing inward. Place a balancing rose quartz on your heart chakra, which is located in the middle of your chest. (A rose quartz pendant on a twenty-four- to twenty-seven-inch chain will generally hang in the correct position if you are sitting up.) Next, while letting your arms drop to your sides, hold in each hand a single terminated clear quartz crystal that you have programmed to be smoky quartz. Point the tips toward the earth. Close your eyes and imagine that you are enveloped in an aura of gentle, earth-colored light.

3. Now, shift your focus to your breathing. Without straining, take a deep, peaceful inhale, imagining the breath entering through the rose quartz and into your heart center. Next, let your breath release as you say the sound *ah*, silently or aloud, as if you are sighing in relief. Imagine that the brown, earthen-colored energy flows from the crystals into the earth as you relax. Continue doing this, gathering peace into your heart center and then letting the gentle brown light flow deeply into the earth. Relax your feet, lower legs, the back of your knees, your upper legs, pelvis, belly, and the small of your back as you let roots of brown light stretch ever downward. Release any disturbing thoughts or feelings, using the same visualization. Perform this procedure for eleven minutes, gradually working your way up to half an hour as you become more practiced.

4. When you are finished, slowly open your eyes. Place the crystals in your hands down beside you, and then remove the crystals that surround you. Remove the rose quartz on your heart center last.

Black Tourmaline Or Onyx

THE PROTECTION CRYSTALS

All black crystals or stones provide protection. Black tourmaline, an essential crystal for your crystal healing kit, is an exceptionally powerful crystal. It not only is useful for protection, but also functions as a potent banishing crystal that will help you release any amount or type of negativity (physical, mental, emotional, psychic, and even spiritual). Whereas turquoise releases negativity through absorption, black tourmaline fiercely projects it away from the subtle body. Black tourmaline can release negative emotional and psychic cords that anyone has used to intentionally or unintentionally bind us to negative or harmful relationships. We can stop mental, emotional, and psychic attacks by surrounding ourselves with a protective aura of black tourmaline. We can wield black tourmaline like a wand to draw negativity out of ourselves and send it into the earth, where it will be transmuted into positivity.

Black onyx is also a deeply grounding stone. Just like black tourmaline, it can help us eliminate unwanted energies that mentally, emotionally, physically, or psychically drain us of energy. When black onyx is placed on the belly between the second and third chakras, it can be used to prevent the energy drain that makes us sick and unwell. Both black tourmaline and black onyx bring deep introspection and allow us to fearlessly gaze into the shadows of our psyche or into the group psyche of the planet. Combined with amethyst and lapis, azurite, or deep blue sapphire, both black tourmaline and black onyx can be used to increase our psychic abilities.

Here is a crystal healing for protection and for banishing negative energy cords that bind us. Removing those draining ties will restore our general vitality and eliminate the subtle cause of illness or disease.

BLACK TOURMALINE FOR BANISHING NEGATIVE ENERGY

1. Lie down on your back or sit upright. Surround yourself with four or eight clear quartz crystals with their tips pointing away from your body. Imagine that they connect with each other to form a circle of bright, powerful, radiant energy. The more clearly you can visualize this, the more powerful the surrounding aura will be.

2. Next, place a double terminated quartz crystal on your heart chakra, located in the middle of your chest. If you are sitting, you can wear a double terminated quartz crystal in a gold or gold-filled setting to bring the energizing power of fire and sun. This will shield your heart so that any negativity released through this healing will be fiercely repelled.

3. When you have your shield firmly visualized and in place, place a black tourmaline or black onyx crystal on your navel point (belly button), midway between your third and second chakras. If it is a single terminated crystal, point the tip down toward the earth. Now place four more clear quartz crystals around the black crystal with their tips pointing outward from it. Place one of the quartz crystals above the stone, one below, and one on each side in a cross-like formation. In your right hand, hold a single terminated clear quartz programmed with black energy. That will help you draw out and expel any unwanted energy that you discover. Hold a double terminated quartz crystal in your left hand to help bring you the information that you need.

4. Close your eyes and visualize that the protective shield formed by the stones repels any negative energy that you sense coming toward you or trying to enter you. If you have a particular situation, disease, or person that comes to mind, imagine that their energy is repelled from your body, mind, emotions, and psyche as it tries to enter.

5. The next step is to actually banish whatever negative energy has gathered within you, whether it is physical, mental, emotional, or psychic. As you do so, know that your protective shield will not only repel negative energies from entering but also expel any banished, negative energies through its permeable barrier. With your eyes still closed, scan your body, feeling or sensing where negativity might lie. Imagine or envision where any black energy cords bind you. See in your mind's eye any person or situation that is psychically lodged within you. Scan your body for any illness or disease that may be reflective of negativity. Sense or envision if and where you are possibly being attacked.

6. As you discover each of these areas within you, use the crystal in your right hand to gather or pull out the negative energy and toss it outside of your protective shield. Envision the negativity sinking into the earth, where it will be transmuted into positivity. Continue until each area seems clear. You will get a definite sense of this. Before moving on to the next location in the body, visualize that a beam of energy from your protective shield flows into this area to fill it with protective and healing light.

7. Once you feel as if you have addressed every area that needs to be cleared of negativity, place the crystals in your hands beside you and rest for at least three minutes with your eyes closed, inhaling and exhaling through your heart chakra. Envision yourself as clear and peaceful, resting within an aura of clear, healing light.

8. When you are finished, open your eyes and remove the rest of the crystals in the reverse order in which you placed them. Be especially mindful to thoroughly clear the crystals that you used in this healing so that any residual negative energy doesn't return to you.

Chapter 6
HEALING CRYSTALS FOR YOUR CRYSTAL HEALING KIT

The following is a list of crystals and stones that you may want to use to augment your basic crystal healing kit. I have grouped them by their color, the degree of heat or coolness that they bring to the subtle body, and the chakra with which they are associated. I have also suggested some emotional and physical healing qualities that they possess. You will find that many similarly colored crystals or stones have comparable healing qualities, enabling them to treat many of the same maladies. When choosing between such stones, select the crystal you are most strongly drawn to.

For your general information, I have also included healing properties that others have channeled through these stones (although I may not choose to do so). As with any crystal, if you feel drawn to a certain stone, try it and see if it works for you.

UPPER CHAKRAS

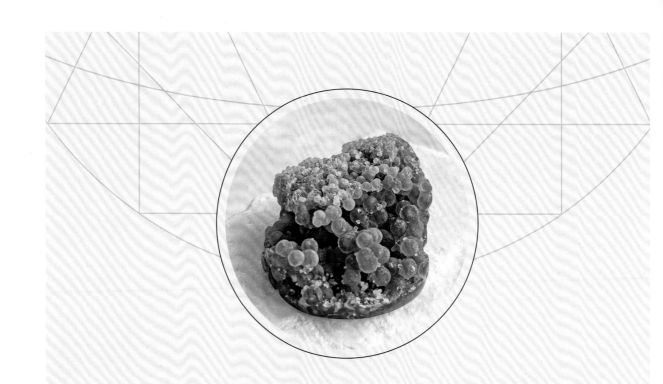

PURPLE CHALCEDONY

CHAKRA: Crown and third eye chakras		
COLOR: Soft violet	CLARITY: Opaque	TEMPERATURE: Cooling
PHYSICAL HEALING QUALITIES: Transmutes negativity for general healing; works with general health, tumors, and infections of the brain; reduces inflammation of optic nerves and eyes; purifies energy fields		
EMOTIONAL HEALING QUALITIES: Uplifting and expansive; calms neurosis and other emotional upsets		

CHAROITE

CHAKRA: Crown and third eye chakras, and somewhat the heart chakra		
COLOR: Purple, violet, sometimes with pink tones	CLARITY: Opaque, sometimes with chatoyancy (color shifts with light)	TEMPERATURE: Cooling

PHYSICAL HEALING QUALITIES: Uplifting; transmutes negativity for general healing.; adds grounding to balance and enhance upper chakra work; cleanses aura, eases pain, tension, headaches, and migraines; calms excess electrical energy in the brain to treat seizures, epilepsy, and meningitis; works more forcefully and with greater accompanying grounding than purple chalcedony, purple jade, sugilite, and fluorite

EMOTIONAL HEALING QUALITIES: Brings clarity and insight; builds self-esteem

CHANNELED HEALING INFORMATION: Regulates blood pressure and pulse (NOTE: I would use chrysocolla, pink kunzite or rose quartz, and red stones for this purpose; they are more traditionally related to blood, circulation, and pulse)

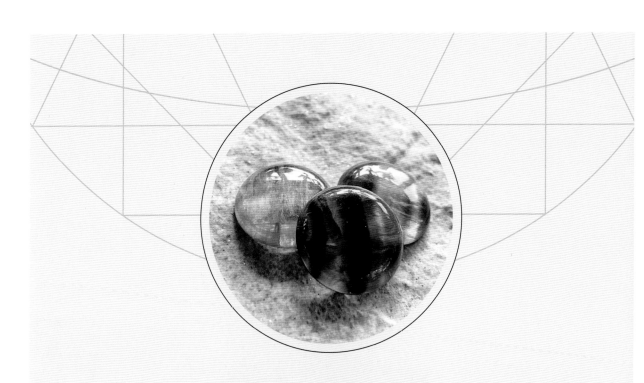

FLUORITE

CHAKRA: Works gently with crown (purple and white), third eye (blue), throat (turquoise), heart (pink and green), and navel point (yellow); mixed colors work on more than one chakra at the same time.

COLOR: Light to deep purple, often mixed with green, blue, yellow, white, or pink	CLARITY: Transparent, translucent, and opaque	TEMPERATURE: Generally cooling

PHYSICAL HEALING QUALITIES: Very soft, uplifting, and energetically soothing; violet works with head injuries, brain tumors, seizures, epilepsy, meningitis, ears, and jaw tension; blue works with mucus membranes and respiratory tract (colds, flu, emphysema, pneumonia); green soothes nerve pain, ulcers, skin sores, staph infections, and shingles; white strengthens bones and teeth, and it treats ulcers; yellow calms nerves and nervous disorders

EMOTIONAL HEALING QUALITIES: All colors, especially pink and green, work with emotional stability, relationship harmony, and calming anxiety

PURPLE JADE

CHAKRA: Crown chakra		
COLOR: Light to dark violet	CLARITY: Opaque	TEMPERATURE: Cooling if light color; slightly warming if dark

PHYSICAL HEALING QUALITIES: Gentle and soothing; enhances innate healing abilities; boosts physical resistance; soothes tension headaches, and migraines; reduces seizures, epilepsy, and any health issues in brain; eases ear aches, jaw tension, and eye problems

EMOTIONAL HEALING QUALITIES: Helps resolve emotional issues by calming the mind and bringing understanding between people

CHANNELED HEALING QUALITIES: Helps heal kidney problems, fluid retention, and blood-sugar imbalances (NOTE: I tend to combine yellow abdominal crystals and green crystals instead. That is due to the fact that fluid balance is largely controlled by the kidneys, which are located in the abdomen, and the heart-related cardiovascular system. The pancreas, located in the abdominal area, controls blood-sugar levels. Be aware: Much purple jade is dyed and won't work the same as the natural stone)

PURPLE KUNZITE
(SPODUMENE)

CHAKRA: Crown chakra		
COLOR: Light violet	CLARITY: Transparent, translucent, and opaque	TEMPERATURE: Cooling

PHYSICAL HEALING QUALITIES: Extremely gentle; clears aura of negative energy that brings illness; removes resistance to all healing; releases blockages in organs, circulatory system, and elsewhere; relieves stress-related illnesses, neuralgia, neuropathy, and neuritis; balances energy of parasympathetic nervous system for better metabolism, digestion, and relaxation; channels feminine energy and etheric spirituality for healing insight

EMOTIONAL HEALING QUALITIES: Uplifting and inspirational; combines intellect with intuition and logic to deepen relationships and tolerance

CHANNELED HEALING QUALITIES: Restructures DNA to heal at the most basic levels; balances hormones

SUGILITE

CHAKRA: Crown and heart chakras		
COLOR: Deep purple to pink	CLARITY: Opaque	TEMPERATURE: Slightly cooling or slightly warming

PHYSICAL HEALING QUALITIES: Calming; connects the spiritual with the physical for diagnostic wisdom; balances brain hemispheres; relieves headaches, pain, inflammation, and arthritis; reduces excess electrical activity in the brain to calm epilepsy and seizures; improves cardiovascular issues

EMOTIONAL HEALING QUALITIES: Connects the wisdom of the heart with the insight of the crown for emotional balance, relational understanding, and establishment of personal boundaries; helps heal heartbreak; brings healing information from astral planes; promotes lucid dreaming.

CHANNELED HEALING QUALITIES: May help with cancer and viruses

AZURITE

CHAKRA: Third eye chakra		
COLOR: Deep royal blue, sometimes combined with green malachite	CLARITY: Opaque to somewhat translucent	TEMPERATURE: Cooling

PHYSICAL HEALING QUALITIES: Relieves negative thought patterns that promote disease; generates brain cells and stimulates brain activity; helps control random and disorganized thoughts of Alzheimer's disease; activates nerve cells in the brain to help Parkinson's disease and other neuro-degenerative diseases of the brain; opens third eye to contact spiritual or angelic guides for spiritual healing (NOTE: The malachite's copper content can treat spine and vertebrae issues, especially when combined with white howlite)

EMOTIONAL HEALING QUALITIES: Controls stressful and negative thoughts to reduce mental trauma; strengthens sense of identity; aids concentration

CHANNELED HEALING QUALITIES: Stimulates growth of embryo; circulates oxygen in body; helps with diseases of the throat and autoimmune disorders

DUMORTIERITE

CHAKRA: Third eye with some earth element if black or gray		
COLOR: Royal blue, sometimes with black or gray areas	CLARITY: Opaque	TEMPERATURE: Cooling
PHYSICAL HEALING QUALITIES: Calming; increases intuitive and psychic abilities to aid diagnosis; adds some earth element to help clear thinking; calms nausea, pain, and cramping; boosts glandular and endocrine health		
EMOTIONAL HEALING QUALITIES: Calms emotional hypersensitivity, bringing emotional perspective for patience and trust; helps relationships; increases mental skills		
CHANNELED HEALING QUALITIES: Relives vomiting (NOTE: This is true only for "nervous stomach"); helps skin disorders, thyroid, and parathyroid problems; eases sunburn; treats depression and carpal tunnel syndrome; relieves colic (NOTE: Instead, I use crystals for intestinal issues)		

IOLITE

CHAKRA: Third eye and crown chakras		
COLOR: Royal blue and violet, depending on light	CLARITY: Opaque, translucent, clear	TEMPERATURE: Cooling
PHYSICAL HEALING QUALITIES: Builds inner strength to enhance immune system; relieves tension headaches; balances and adds vitality to metabolism; balances hemispheres of the brain to harmonize male/female energies; can aid weight loss and release the causes of addiction through positive visualization; good inner-journey crystal to bring healing		
EMOTIONAL HEALING QUALITIES: Stimulates imagination to increase personal capabilities and self-expression; calms the mind; brings insight and creativity		
CHANNELED HEALING QUALITIES: Eliminates fatty deposits; treats fevers		

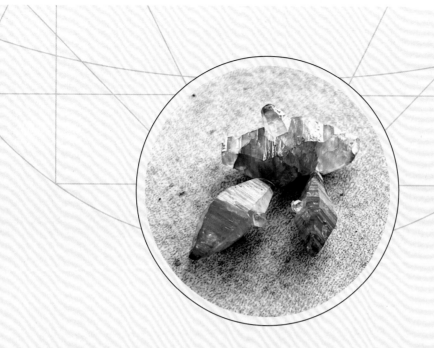

BLUE SAPPHIRE

CHAKRA: Third eye chakra	
COLOR: Dark royal blue to powder blue	CLARITY: Opaque to clear

PHYSICAL HEALING QUALITIES: Protective; increases intuition and meditation to aid diagnosis; helps release depression (light blue); eliminates negative energies from aura; overall tonic for good health and well-being; eases insomnia, nightmares, and sleeping problems; calms overactive body systems

EMOTIONAL HEALING QUALITIES: Connects to the higher self for emotional perspective, serenity, and peace of mind; releases mental tension and confusion; acts as a prosperity stone; brings generosity and optimism; increases loyalty

CHANNELED HEALING QUALITIES: Treats blood disorders, excessive bleeding, and cellular disorders; regulates glands; thickens walls of veins; relieves sleep apnea

CELESTITE

CHAKRA: Third eye and throat chakras		
COLOR: Light powder blue with white	CLARITY: Slightly opaque to transparent	TEMPERATURE: Cooling

PHYSICAL HEALING QUALITIES: Connects with psychic, angelic, and astral realms for healing assistance; calms fevers and pain; relieves headaches, earaches, eye problems, teeth grinding, and tight jaw and scalp; treats teeth, top of the spinal cord, bones, muscles, ligaments, and other soft tissues; helps broken bones knit; treats any lung issue, including tumors, respiration, pneumonia, colds, and respiratory symptoms; relieves stress to help digestive and skin problems; releases blockages in the physical, mental, and emotional bodies

EMOTIONAL HEALING QUALITIES: Soothing; calms anger; brings hope, joy, and inspiration; elevates spirit and mind, instills a healing perspective for emotional issues

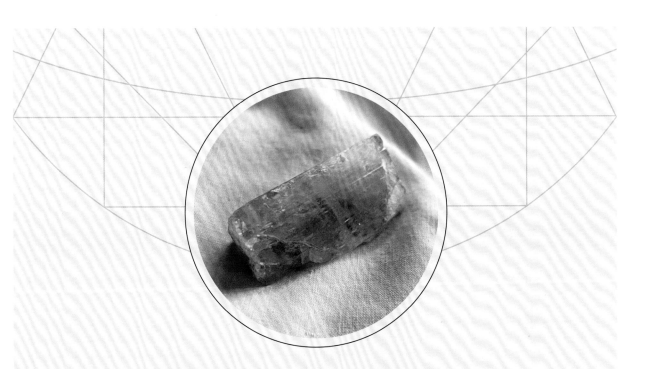

BLUE KUNZITE
(SPODUMENE)

CHAKRA: Third eye and throat chakras		
COLOR: Light powder blue	CLARITY: Opaque to transparent	TEMPERATURE: Cooling

PHYSICAL HEALING QUALITIES: Works on jaw and cranium, teeth, top of spine, and bones, especially when combined with white howlite or selenite; relieves sore throats, stiff necks and joints, laryngitis, bronchial conditions, emphysema, and lung damage; alleviates stress and anxiety conditions felt in the solar plexus

EMOTIONAL HEALING QUALITIES: Connects to spiritual and angelic realms; eases sadness, depression, loneliness, fear, and uncertainty; helps release emotional effects of trauma, including PTSD; brings emotional equilibrium through balanced heart and mind; enhances ability to love through connection to divine love; instills comfort, deep calm, and inner peace; reduces depression

CHANNELED HEALING QUALITIES: May help relieve some forms of mental illness

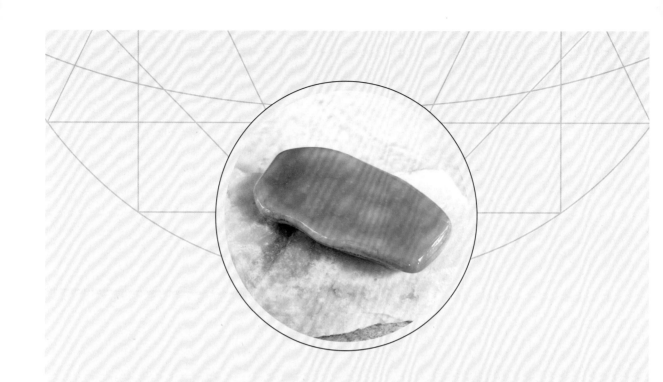

BLUE QUARTZ

CHAKRA: Third eye and throat chakras, with some earth influence		
COLOR: Medium blue, sometimes with darker dumortierite within	CLARITY: Opaque to translucent	TEMPERATURE: Cooling
PHYSICAL HEALING QUALITIES: Detoxifying; helps tonsillitis, throat problems, tinnitus and hearing; stimulates pituitary gland to regulate the thyroid, adrenal, ovarian, and testicular glands; assists in releasing hormones into the blood; balances blood pressure; stimulates pineal gland for melatonin production and better sleep; calms hyperactivity		
EMOTIONAL HEALING QUALITIES: Brings clarity, focus, optimism, decisiveness, serenity, and insight; improves communication; aids compromise		

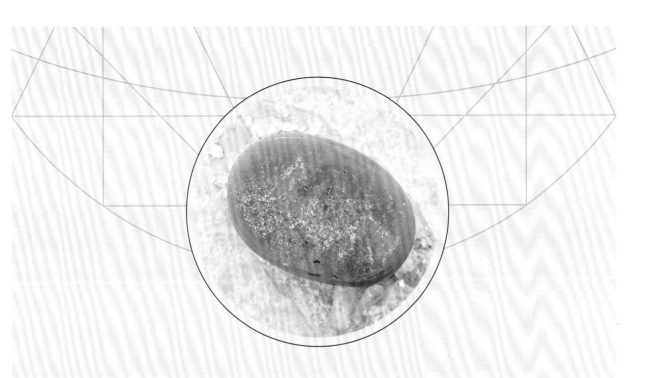

AMAZONITE

CHAKRA: Throat and, if green-toned, heart chakras		
COLOR: Turquoise or turquoise-green	CLARITY: Opaque	TEMPERATURE: Cooling
PHYSICAL HEALING QUALITIES: Relaxes muscle spasms, nervous system, and overactive brain activity; calms pain and swelling of gout, rheumatism, arthritis, and skin irritations; eases calcium deficiency and osteoporosis; treats throat, lungs, respiration, and bronchial passages		
EMOTIONAL HEALING QUALITIES: Blue-green color aids loving expression; helps relieve stubbornness and bring flexibility in relationship; instills hope and tranquility		

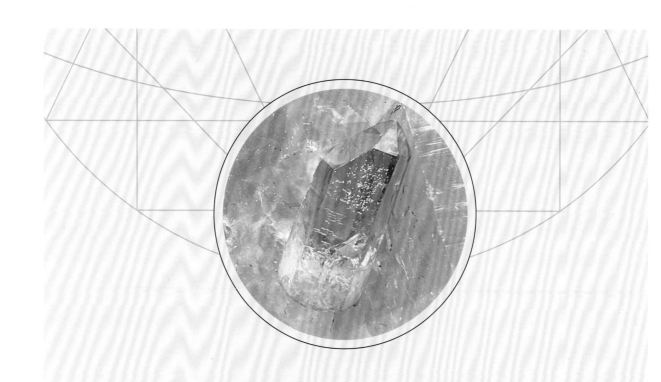

AQUA AURA

CHAKRA: Crown and throat chakras		
COLOR: Turquoise blue with rainbow flashes	CLARITY: Transparent	TEMPERATURE: Cooling or slightly warming

PHYSICAL HEALING QUALITIES: A clear quartz crystal bonded with pure gold, it is highly energetic; charges electromagnetic field and clears it of impurities; enhances basic life force in all organs; strengthens immune system and decreases fever; stimulates pineal, thymus, and thyroid glands; balances male/female energies of body for optimal functioning; can rapidly transform the negative energy that supports illness

EMOTIONAL HEALING QUALITIES: Illuminating and uplifting; connects with angelic realms; brings inner stillness, joy, and peace; reduces panic, anxiety, and anger; enhances communication

CHANNELED HEALING QUALITIES: Good for distance healing (NOTE: All crystals can be used in distance healing.); brings wealth and prosperity (NOTE: Instead, I would use green or light yellow/gold crystals); works with pancreas, liver, and spleen

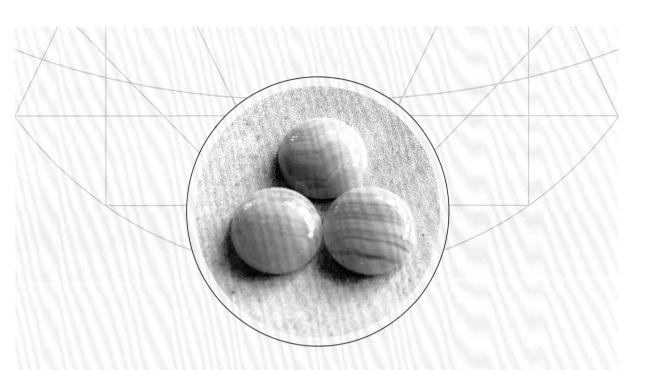

BLUE LACE AGATE
(CHALCEDONY)

CHAKRA: Throat chakra		
COLOR: Baby blue with white streaks	CLARITY: Opaque	TEMPERATURE: Cooling
PHYSICAL HEALING QUALITIES: High quartz content energizes; copper and white-blue color calms and enhances immune system; treats throat, thyroid, teeth, and bones; improves skin and calms inflammation; stimulates lymph nodes of neck, jaw, and collarbone to fight infection; helps clear lungs and aids respiration; decreases anxiety to lower blood pressure		
EMOTIONAL HEALING QUALITIES: Instills soothing, calming, clarity, self-perspective, and optimism; helps communicate inner truth		

CHRYSOCOLLA

CHAKRA: Throat and heart chakras, added earth influence if it contains black or brown		
COLOR: Green and turquoise, sometimes with brown or black	CLARITY: Opaque	TEMPERATURE: Cooling to slightly warming
PHYSICAL HEALING QUALITIES: Brings earth element to work on structural system; copper content helps fight infections; water element aids in the release of blockages; absorbs negativity that causes illness; strengthens physical, cardiovascular, and circulatory systems; heals throat conditions; relieves pain		
EMOTIONAL HEALING QUALITIES: Instills sense of security to alleviate vulnerability; enhances focus and controls scattered emotions; facilitates communication; eases fear		

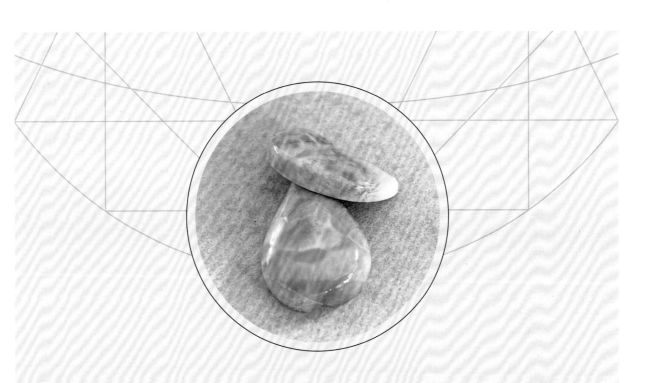

LARIMAR

CHAKRA: Throat chakra		
COLOR: Light turquoise with white	CLARITY: Opaque	TEMPERATURE: Cooling

PHYSICAL HEALING QUALITIES: Associated with sky and water; calms and soothes all physical, mental, and emotional upset; releases negativity and improves underlying ill health; treats bones of cranium and upper spine; helps heal throat, soft tissue, pineal gland, and associated organs

EMOTIONAL HEALING QUALITIES: Uplifting; calms stress and anxiety; reduces negativity; equalizes emotional extremes; eases bipolar disorder and anxiety-related mental disorders; relieves stubbornness; enhances communication

TURQUOISE OPAL

CHAKRA: Throat chakra	
CLARITY: Opaque to translucent	TEMPERATURE: Slightly warming
PHYSICAL HEALING QUALITIES: Works with light body to speed healing; releases physical, emotional, and mental blockages; improves physical vitality and strengthens life force; water and air element calms respiratory inflammation, lung damage, asthma, and chronic coughs; treats throat, eyes, kidneys, and hydration issues	
EMOTIONAL HEALING QUALITIES: Uplifting and joyful; intensifies emotions and releases inhibitions; stimulates creativity, dreams, passion, spontaneity, and independence	

HEART
CHAKRA

CHRYSOPRASE
(GREEN CHALCEDONY)

CHAKRA: Heart chakra, sometimes with some earth influence		
COLOR: Light to dark green, blue-green or yellow-green, with brown or white quartz	CLARITY: Opaque	TEMPERATURE: Cooling
PHYSICAL HEALING QUALITIES: Aligns the energies of the heart with the solar plexus and throat—degree of alignment determined by color; brings vitality into body; counteracts exhaustion; soothes digestive issues and some skin conditions; aids general detox; if yellow-toned, can stimulate liver and help filter blood; treats heart and stress-related conditions; strengthens heart muscle; regulates pulse		
EMOTIONAL HEALING QUALITIES: Instills love, joy, hope, and nurturing; calms troubled emotions		

EMERALD

CHAKRA: Heart chakra		
COLOR: Bright green	CLARITY: Transparent or translucent	TEMPERATURE: Warming
PHYSICAL HEALING QUALITIES: Very strong heart-centered healing; works with any heart problems; helps blood-related issues, circulation, and blood pressure; channels strong nurturing healing energy for any illness or disease		
EMOTIONAL HEALING QUALITIES: Immediate and strong heart opening qualities; increases capacity for love, self-acceptance, empathy, and compassion; spreads joy and lightness of spirit; instills a sense of prosperity and good fortune		

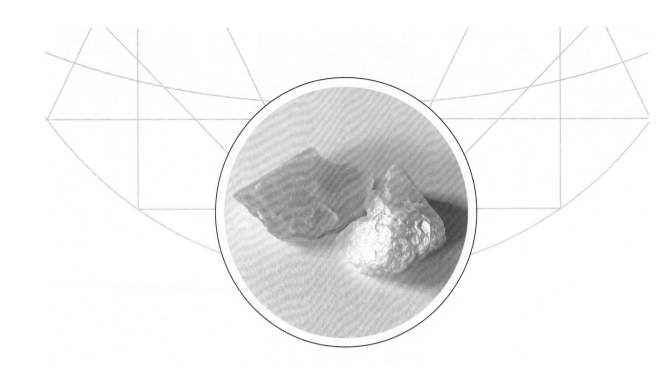

GREEN KUNZITE
(SPODUMENE OR HIDDENITE)

CHAKRA: Heart chakra		
COLOR: Bright green, light green, or light yellow-green	CLARITY: Opaque, translucent, or transparent	TEMPERATURE: Cooling
PHYSICAL HEALING QUALITIES: Inclusion of lithium makes it physically, emotionally, and mentally relaxing; calms heart arrhythmia; counteracts fire-like conditions such as fever, injury, or physical trauma; improves stress-related illnesses; treats heart; nurtures physical body; eases arthritis and other inflammatory conditions		
EMOTIONAL HEALING QUALITIES: Dissolves relationship issues; instills a sense of safety and total self-acceptance amid vulnerability; amplifies love, compassion, empathy, mutual understanding, and acceptance		
CHANNELED HEALING QUALITIES: Helps with eating disorders, bulimia, anorexia, and body dysmorphia		

PINK KUNZITE
(SPODUMENE)

CHAKRA: Heart and crown chakras		
COLOR: Pink	CLARITY: Opaque, translucent, or transparent	TEMPERATURE: Gently warming
PHYSICAL HEALING QUALITIES: Stimulates heart chakra and muscle; enhances circulatory system; soothes muscular tension, sciatica, arthritis, and joint pain; cleanses aura of impurities and negative energy that underlies illness		
EMOTIONAL HEALING QUALITIES: Releases emotional barriers; instills tolerance, ability to accept criticism, compassion, empathy, and love; lifts mood and counteracts depression; aligns the heart chakra with higher chakras to enhance wisdom and perspective		
CHANNELED HEALING QUALITIES: Helps produce blood corpuscles; prevents narrowing of the arteries		

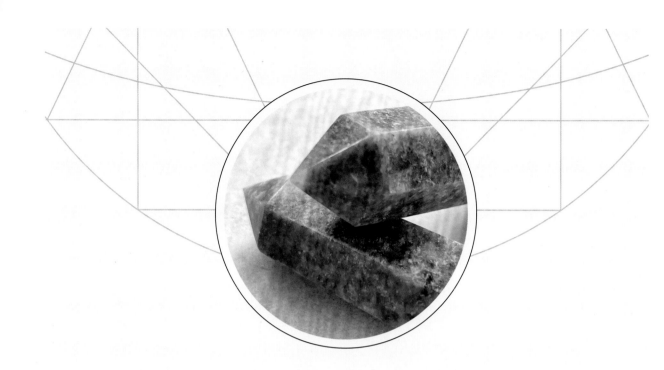

LEPIDOLITE

CHAKRA: Heart and crown chakras		
COLOR: Predominately pink with violet, gray, and white	CLARITY: Opaque	TEMPERATURE: Cooling
PHYSICAL HEALING QUALITIES: Known as the "valium of the crystal world," it is extremely calming; brings wisdom of the upper planes to join the heart for diagnosis; calms hypervigilance, hyperactivity, overexcited brain activity, muscular tension, cramping, irritable bowel syndrome, ulcers, skin lesions, and rashes; treats diseases related to anxiety and stress		
EMOTIONAL HEALING QUALITIES: Quick calming for emergency situations; the "rescue remedy" of crystals; instills love, compassion, tolerance, empathy, universal love, and spiritual wisdom		

PERIDOT

(CHRYSOLITE)

CHAKRA: Heart chakra, with some earth (volcanic) energy		
COLOR: Olive or yellow-green	CLARITY: Transparent	TEMPERATURE: Warming
PHYSICAL HEALING QUALITIES: Eases stomach aches, sore muscles, and body aches; because of yellow undertones, improves digestive system and abdominal maladies; slows heart palpitations and helps heart conditions		
EMOTIONAL HEALING QUALITIES: Instills confidence and sense of good fortune; brings calm during crisis; wards off emotional darkness; channels illumination provided by natural world; calms despair; brings grounding stability		
CHANNELED HEALING QUALITIES: Attracts wealth and brings good luck; sharpens eyesight; helps bruised ribs; eases respiratory issues		

RHODONITE

CHAKRA: Heart chakra, with earth energies		
COLOR: Pink with gray	CLARITY: Opaque	TEMPERATURE: Gently warming
PHYSICAL HEALING QUALITIES: Relaxing; deeply calms the physical body; balances male and female energies; helps heal heart-related illnesses; increases physical strength; treats lungs and respiratory systems; eases emphysema; stimulates thymus gland and lymph system; improves blood circulation		
EMOTIONAL HEALING QUALITIES: Opens heart chakra; brings love, empathy, and compassion into the physical body and life; helps establish personal boundaries in relationships; alleviates phobias, panic, and emotional shock		
CHANNELED HEALING QUALITIES: Reduces scarring; aids bones; stimulates fertility; helps heal stomach ulcers		

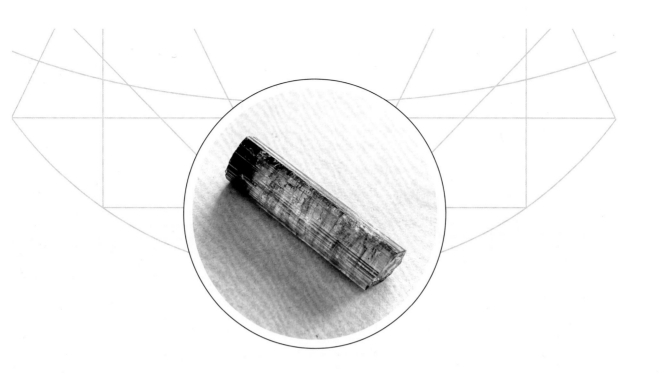

GREEN TOURMALINE

CHAKRA: Heart chakra		
COLOR: Dark to light green	CLARITY: Opaque, translucent, or transparent	TEMPERATURE: Cooling
PHYSICAL HEALING QUALITIES: Relaxes and relieves physical trauma of broken bones, sprains, pulled muscles, muscular tension and cramps, deep cuts and wounds, seizures, and some forms of heart attack; improves heart health; calms indigestion and irritation in organs		
EMOTIONAL HEALING QUALITIES: Brings love, compassion, empathy, acceptance, and nurturing for self and others; connects with nature and natural world to bring peace		

PINK TOURMALINE
(RUBELLITE)

CHAKRA: Heart chakra		
COLOR: Pink	CLARITY: Opaque, translucent, or transparent	TEMPERATURE: Warming
PHYSICAL HEALING QUALITIES: Assists with heart attack recovery; heals any illness or condition related to the physical heart, including angina and irregular heartbeats; if within clear quartz, the effects will be greatly amplified		
EMOTIONAL HEALING QUALITIES: Uplifting; heals emotional wounds; brings inner peace, universal love, and joy; clears aura of emotional pain; combine with black tourmaline or onyx for emotional protection		
CHANNELED HEALING QUALITIES: Helps heal gynecological conditions; regulates menstrual cycle; aids conception		

WATERMELON TOURMALINE

CHAKRA: Heart chakra		
COLOR: Blended pink and green	CLARITY: Opaque, translucent, or transparent	TEMPERATURE: Warming

PHYSICAL HEALING QUALITIES: Blending pink and green brings complete heart-healing capabilities; treats heart disorders and cardiovascular system; boosts immune system; stimulates thymus in children to strengthen immune system; helps regenerate total body system; accelerates all healing, especially when combined with amethyst; relieves pain and stress-related disorders

EMOTIONAL HEALING QUALITIES: Instills compassion, heart-centered awareness, emotional vulnerability, and nurturing energy; balances emotional extremes, including paranoia and hypervigilance; eases grief and brings inner peace and forgiveness; opens heart chakra for empathy, love, truthful living, and compassion

CHANNELED HEALING QUALITIES: Helps adrenals and entire endocrine system; instills sense of prosperity

LOWER CHAKRAS

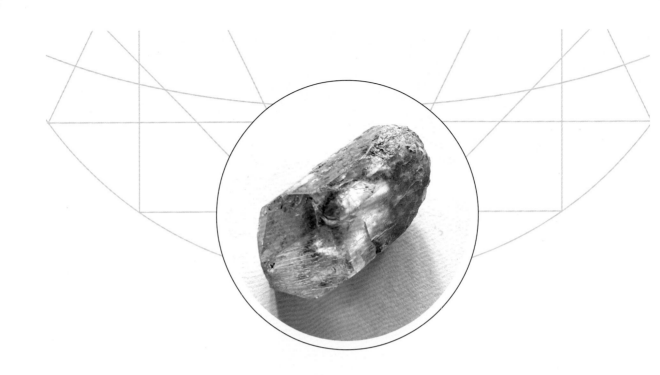

YELLOW APATITE
(CALCIUM PHOSPHATE)

CHAKRA: Third chakra		
COLOR: Bright to pale yellow	CLARITY: Opaque to transparent	TEMPERATURE: Warming
PHYSICAL HEALING QUALITIES: Energizing; stimulates subtle and physical nervous systems; eases chronic fatigue syndrome; treats liver, gallbladder, pancreas, spleen, and stomach; offers some help for bones, teeth, hair, and nails; aids detoxification; boosts immune system		
EMOTIONAL HEALING QUALITIES: Helps manifest desires, removing self-imposed limitations; increases feelings of self-worth and confidence; relieves shyness and depression; builds positive energy field		

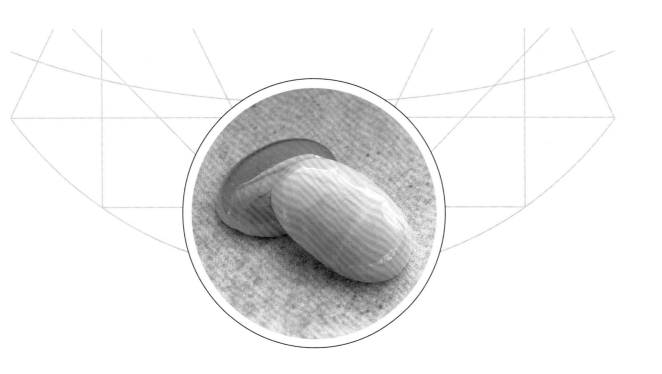

YELLOW ARAGONITE
(TUFA)

CHAKRA: Third chakra, with some earth energy		
COLOR: Pale honey-yellow with white bands, sometimes with brown	CLARITY: Opaque, translucent, or transparent	TEMPERATURE: Warming

PHYSICAL HEALING QUALITIES: Stimulates nerve conduction while relaxing nervous system; promotes gentle healing of stomach and surrounding organs; channels earth energy to strengthen and vitalize all soft tissues, bones, teeth, hair, and fingernails; boosts immune system

EMOTIONAL HEALING QUALITIES: Gently uplifts, bringing joy, optimism, and gentleness; instills emotional strength and helps establish personal boundaries

YELLOW CALCITE

CHAKRA: Third chakra		
COLOR: Yellow	CLARITY: Opaque to transparent	TEMPERATURE: Warming
PHYSICAL HEALING QUALITIES: Gently vitalizes entire body; soothes while vitalizing the subtle and physical nervous systems; calms upset stomach and irritable bowels; heals digestive problems; builds protective energy field around the body to repel the negative energy that underlies ill health		
EMOTIONAL HEALING QUALITIES: Uplifts disposition and helps relieve depression; instills a sense of joy, capability, and power to achieve any goal; protects against personal attack		

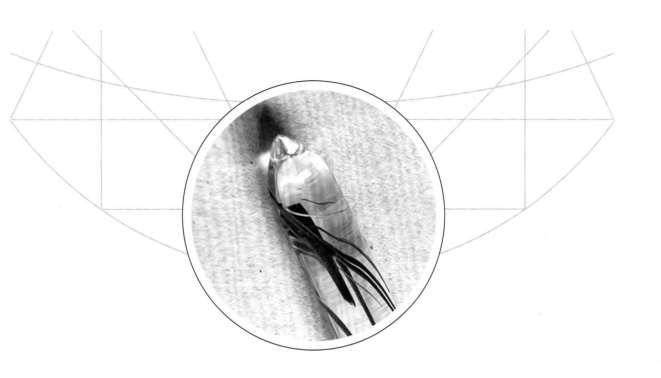

GOLD RUTILATED QUARTZ

CHAKRA: Crown and third chakras		
COLOR: White or clear with gold rutile	CLARITY: Translucent or transparent	TEMPERATURE: Warming
PHYSICAL HEALING QUALITIES: Extremely energizing; used for divination and diagnosis; stimulates subtle and physical nervous systems; offers some help for digestion, bowels, kidneys, spleen, pancreas, blood filtering, and insulin production		
EMOTIONAL HEALING QUALITIES: Instills courage, willpower, optimism, and hope; alleviates fear and depression; boosts intuition and sense of prosperity; channels insight from higher angelic planes		

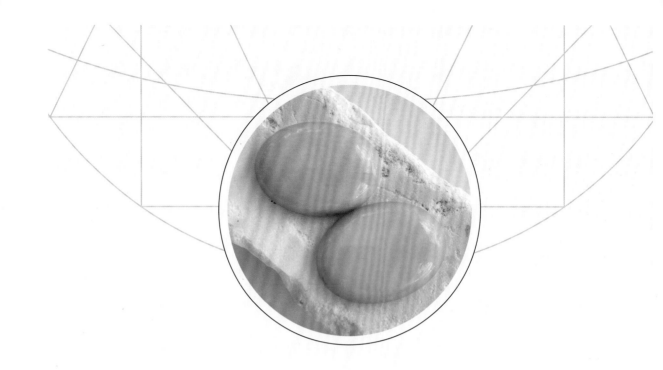

YELLOW JADE
(NEPHRITE)

CHAKRA: Third chakra, with some earth energy if mustard colored		
COLOR: Bright to mustard yellow	CLARITY: Opaque	TEMPERATURE: Warming
PHYSICAL HEALING QUALITIES: Energizes and balances subtle and physical nervous systems and adrenal insufficiency while bringing grounding to calm hyperactivity; vitalizes body; increases strength of will to heal; aids digestion, kidneys, bowels, bladder, spleen, and thymus		
EMOTIONAL HEALING QUALITIES: Instills optimism, courage, enthusiasm, and sense of abundance		
CHANNELED HEALING QUALITIES: Stimulates intellect; heals larynx; increases blood circulation		

YELLOW TIGER EYE
(QUARTZ)

CHAKRA: Third and earth chakras		
COLOR: Yellow with brown streaks, chatoyant (color shifts with light)	CLARITY: Opaque	TEMPERATURE: Warming

PHYSICAL HEALING QUALITIES: Strengthens subtle and physical nervous systems while calming; provides physical strength for the body; calms panic and anxiety; relieves stomach issues; channels earth energy to strengthen the activity of the soft tissues, stomach, liver, pancreas, spleen, and thymus area; regulates blood flow and pulse, especially if paired with green crystals

EMOTIONAL HEALING QUALITIES: Instills immediate courage, motivation, self-trust, willpower, and a strong sense of capability; helps establish strong personal boundaries and emotional protection from narcissism, emotional manipulation, rage, gaslighting, borderline personality disorder, and interpersonal attack

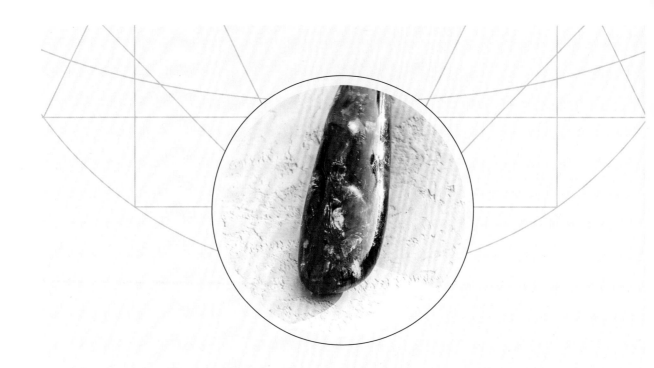

YELLOW AND ORANGE AMBER
(FOSSILIZED TREE RESIN)

CHAKRA: Third and second chakras		
COLOR: Yellow to orange	CLARITY: Opaque to translucent	TEMPERATURE: Warming
PHYSICAL HEALING QUALITIES: Gently vitalizing; known as the "woman's stone"; treats all female-related health issues, including reproductive difficulties and problems with the ovaries, uterus, and pelvis; helps with easier birth; draws disease out of stomach and organs near the stomach; treats the endocrine system and hormones; eases pain		
EMOTIONAL HEALING QUALITIES: Draws out emotional trauma; releases negative energy, anxiety, negative self-judgment, phobias, and fear-related conditions; promotes joy, creativity, comfort, mothering energy, and manifesting ability; balances emotional extremes		
CHANNELED HEALING QUALITIES: Brings psychic protection (NOTE: Clear quartz and black stones will protect more efficiently)		

ORANGE (RED) AVENTURINE
(QUARTZ)

CHAKRA: Second chakra		
COLOR: Pale to bright orange	CLARITY: Opaque to translucent	TEMPERATURE: Quite warming
PHYSICAL HEALING QUALITIES: Assists with pregnancy; treats all female-related health conditions, including ectopic pregnancies, infertility, reoccurring miscarriages, endometriosis, and problems with the ovaries and uterus; treats prostate, testes, kidneys, and urogenital system; can help with uterine and prostate cancer		
EMOTIONAL HEALING QUALITIES: Increases eroticism and sensuality; releases inhibitions, self-criticism, timidity, and shyness; builds self-confidence, perseverance, determination, creativity, and manifestation ability		

ORANGE CALCITE

CHAKRA: Second chakra (sun and fire)		
COLOR: Pale to bright orange and yellow-orange	CLARITY: Opaque to translucent	TEMPERATURE: Very warming
PHYSICAL HEALING QUALITIES: Brings gentle healing vitality; clears negative energy; balances three lower chakras, especially stimulating second and third chakras; heals gynecological problems, ectopic pregnancies, infertility, miscarriages, prostate and testicular diseases, endometriosis, ovarian cysts, urinary tract, and kidneys; increases libido in both men and women; soothes and heals stomach, liver, pancreas, and hormonal system, especially when combined with a yellow crystal		
EMOTIONAL HEALING QUALITIES: Instills peace, joy, happiness, positivity, perseverance, decisiveness, and actualization; facilitates erotic, loving sensuality		
CHANNELED HEALING QUALITIES: Increases intuition and psychic development; helps skin care; protects from radiation and EMF rays		

ORANGE KYANITE

(SPUDOMEME)

CHAKRA: Second chakra		
COLOR: Orange to orange-brown.	CLARITY: Opaque, translucent, or transparent	TEMPERATURE: Warming

PHYSICAL HEALING QUALITIES: Works with reproduction, ovaries and uterus, gynecological problems, pregnancy, infertility, reoccurring miscarriages, endometriosis, and ovarian cysts; increases sex drive; heals or prevents urinary and kidney problems and gall stones; relieves lower back pain

EMOTIONAL HEALING QUALITIES: Increases eroticism; stimulates creativity, pleasure, and imagination; somewhat tranquilizing due to manganese composition

CHANNELED HEALING QUALITIES: Helps conquer addiction; charges DNA with etheric energy; increases clairsentience.

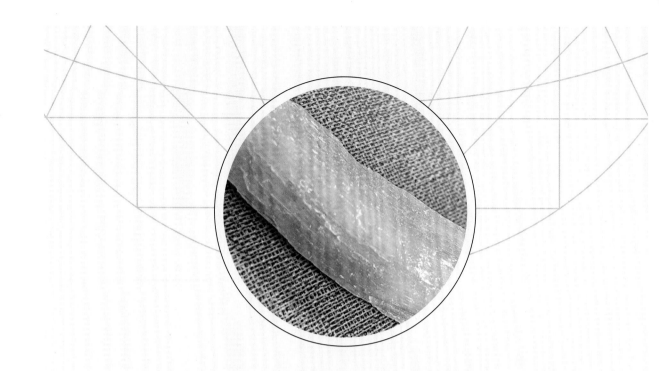

ORANGE (RED) SELENITE
(SATIN SPAR, GYPSUM)

CHAKRA: Second and crown chakras, with earth and moon energies		
COLOR: Bright to pale orange or red-orange (deeper red selenite is almost always dyed)	CLARITY: Opaque to translucent	TEMPERATURE: Gently warming

PHYSICAL HEALING QUALITIES: Adds gentle grounding quality to all second chakra healing; aids gynecological problems, infertility, endometriosis, and ovaries; assists with pregnancy; heals or prevents urinary and kidney problems and gallstones; relieves lower back pain; treats lower spine, hips, and pelvis; offers some help with soft tissue

EMOTIONAL HEALING QUALITIES: Boosts self-esteem and sense of well-being; enhances creativity, eroticism, and pleasure; helps manifest dreams and desires; channels angelic protection; expands intuition and awareness of higher self

CHANNELED HEALING QUALITIES: Helps heal epilepsy

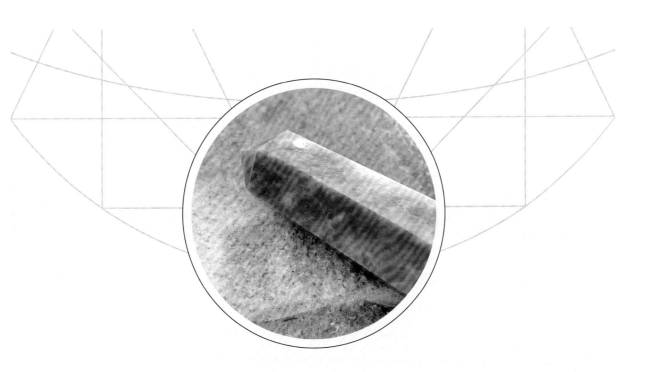

ORANGE SUNSTONE
(FELDSPAR)

CHAKRA: Related primarily to second and first chakras		
COLOR: Orange or red-orange	CLARITY: Opaque, translucent, or transparent	TEMPERATURE: Very warming to hot
PHYSICAL HEALING QUALITIES: Stimulates libido; treats female reproductive system, including uterus, fallopian tubes, and ovaries; assists with pregnancy and infertility; heals or prevents urinary and kidney problems and gallstones; red-orange works with heart and brings strength and vitality		
EMOTIONAL HEALING QUALITIES: Brings personal empowerment, stamina, passion, excitement, sense of self-worth, and happiness; relieves depression and seasonal affective disorder; increases metabolism		
CHANNELED HEALING QUALITIES: Helps heal cartilage, spinal damage, sprains, and muscular pain		

RED AGATE
(CHALCEDONY, QUARTZ, AND SILICA)

CHAKRA: Primarily first chakra, some heart chakra and earth influence		
COLOR: Red, often with black, brown, and white swirls	CLARITY: Opaque or translucent	TEMPERATURE: Hot
PHYSICAL HEALING QUALITIES: Brings universal life-force energy to entire body; assists physical and emotional heart healing; enables purification; treats male reproductive system; increases male libido; heals conditions of the bottom three vertebrae; treats organs, vessels, veins, and muscles of lower pelvis and perineum; protects against negative energy		
EMOTIONAL HEALING QUALITIES: Instills sense of safety and security to reduce aggression, stubbornness, and rage; offers protection and increases stability		
CHANNELED HEALING QUALITIES: Used for divination and to increase psychic energy. Heals eyes, hearing, epilepsy, skin conditions, and stomach cramps		

BLOODSTONE
(HELIOTROPE)

CHAKRA: First and heart chakras		
COLOR: Deep green, blue-gray, or blue-green, with red spots or swirls	CLARITY: Opaque	TEMPERATURE: Warming
PHYSICAL HEALING QUALITIES: Brings growth, regeneration, and the earth's life force; treats blood, circulation, blood coagulation, blood disorders, blood purifying organs, and perineum; detoxifies liver, spleen, kidneys, and intestines; helps with issues of physical heart muscle; a ground bloodstone poultice may help clear infection and draw out toxins related to tumors and skin ulcers		
EMOTIONAL HEALING QUALITIES: Helps ground higher spiritual awareness to physical reality; instills nurturing and protection; removes emotional confusion; increases confidence, inner security, courage, and motivation		
CHANNELED HEALING QUALITIES: Instills altruism; improves hormone balance in menopausal women; relieves menstrual problems; a poultice will draw out snake venom		

RED CALCITE

CHAKRA: First chakra		
COLOR: Dark to light red, sometimes with white and orange	CLARITY: Opaque to translucent.	TEMPERATURE: Quite warm
PHYSICAL HEALING QUALITIES: Detoxifying; soothes as it gently energizes; helps anus; eases constipation; purifies blood with some anti-cancer and anti-oxidant qualities; increases libido in men and women; treats male reproductive issues; accelerates blood flow and activates muscles in perineum area; soothing and energizing to bones, particularly those of the lower spine, feet, ankles; and legs		
EMOTIONAL HEALING QUALITIES: Brings energy, passion, and protection from negative energy; soothes trauma from sexual abuse; enhances instinct, or "gut feeling"; protects against negative energy; instills feelings of potency, security, and safety; provides solid grounding in root chakra to support rising consciousness		
CHANNELED HEALING QUALITIES: Calms rage		

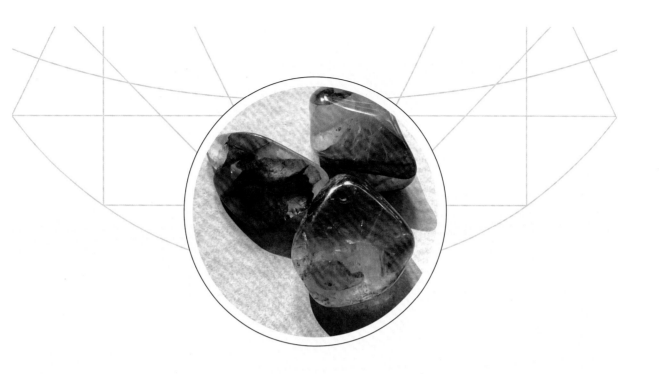

RED HEMATITE

("FIRE QUARTZ," RED QUARTZ, HEMATOID QUARTZ)

CHAKRA: Root and deep earth chakras		
COLOR: Primarily deep red and black, sometimes with gray and white, or as red hematite inclusions in quartz	CLARITY: Opaque, translucent, or transparent	TEMPERATURE: Hot
PHYSICAL HEALING QUALITIES: Strengthens and energizes body; channels earth energy to work with negative conditions of the bones, tissues, and physical structure; composed of oxidized iron, treats anemia, purifies and oxygenates blood; helps wounds heal and tissues regenerate; aids muscles, veins, arteries, and muscles of perineum; heals other root chakra conditions; increases male sexual energy; treats male reproductive system		
EMOTIONAL HEALING QUALITIES: Balances and integrates energies of the spiritual and physical planes; strengthens meditative focus; instills courage and a sense of security and protection		

RED JASPER

CHAKRA: First chakra		
COLOR: Red, sometimes with brown or black striations	CLARITY: Opaque	TEMPERATURE: Very warming
PHYSICAL HEALING QUALITIES: Treats genital/rectal area, male reproductive system, coccyx, perineum, bladder, legs, knees, feet and first three vertebrae of spine; increases vitality and physical strength; alleviates autoimmune disorders, eating disorders, obesity, and basic structural issues		
EMOTIONAL HEALING QUALITIES: Calms hypervigilance; instills sense of basic security and safety; increases survival instincts and "gut level" sense of truth		

RED TIGER EYE
("DRAGON EYE," QUARTZ WITH CROCIDOLITE)

CHAKRA: First and upper earth chakras		
COLOR: Brownish-red, with black or metallic gray streaks	CLARITY: Opaque with chatoyancy (change of color with light)	TEMPERATURE: Hot
PHYSICAL HEALING QUALITIES: Helps heal sexual trauma and abuse; increases libido; treats male reproductive system and erectile dysfunction; boosts physical strength; heals perineum and perineum musculature; treats veins and arteries affecting the soleus muscle, fibula muscle, ankle joints, and big toes; alleviates eating disorders and obesity; energizes sciatic nerve		
EMOTIONAL HEALING QUALITIES: Brings sense of security; increases potency, passion, motivation, and desire		
CHANNELED HEALING QUALITIES: Balances logic and emotions (NOTE: Combining blue with pink or green crystals would be more effective)		

Chapter 7

ADDITIONAL HEALING CRYSTALS FOR YOUR CRYSTAL HEALING KIT

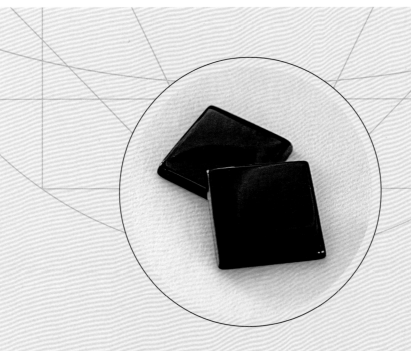

BLACK AGATE AND ONYX
(CHALCEDONY, SILICA, QUARTZ)

CHAKRA: Eighth chakra (three feet below the body into the earth)		
COLOR: Black	CLARITY: Opaque	TEMPERATURE: Cooling
PHYSICAL HEALING QUALITIES: Brings vitalizing energy from deep earth for balanced physical energy; shields from energy drain; protects against contagion; deflects negative physical, mental, and emotional influences; calms excessive nervous energy		
EMOTIONAL HEALING QUALITIES: Prevents emotional energy depletion; provides stability, self-discipline, constancy, and release from fear and worry		
CHANNELED HEALING QUALITIES: Sharpens mind; connects with past life and helps resolve past-life issues		

BROWN ANDRADITE GARNET

CHAKRA: First, foot, and earth chakras		
COLOR: Brown or reddish-brown	CLARITY: Opaque to transparent	TEMPERATURE: Warming
PHYSICAL HEALING QUALITIES: Opens foot chakras to heal insomnia, fatigue, and restlessness; absorbs and regulates life force; treats spine, especially bottom three vertebrae; alleviates impotency; treats male reproductive system		
EMOTIONAL HEALING QUALITIES: Expels negative emotional energies; enhances creativity; instills sense of security and safety; helps realize planetary and universal connection		

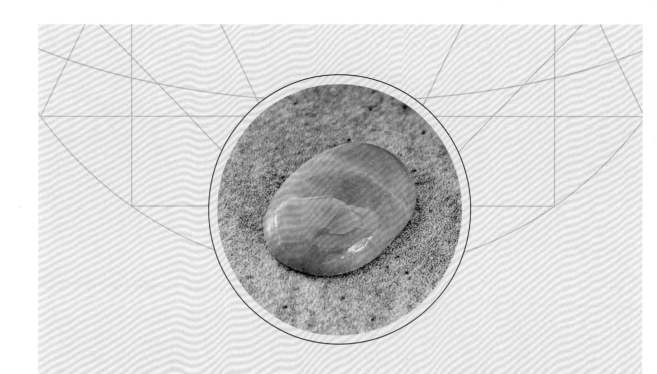

BROWN ARAGONITE
(TUFA)

CHAKRA: Foot and earth chakras		
COLOR: Brown	CLARITY: Opaque or translucent	TEMPERATURE: Cooling
PHYSICAL HEALING QUALITIES: Calming; calcium carbonate composition helps strengthen bones, teeth, nails, and hair; aids in calcium absorption; boosts immune system; decreases fatigue; absorbs and relieves pain; brings energizing life force into body (NOTE: Not good to use for tonic water)		
EMOTIONAL HEALING QUALITIES: Reduces mental, emotional, and physical instability; increases patience, steadiness, and concentration; reduces oversensitive emotions		

HEMATITE
(IRON OXIDE)

CHAKRA: First, third eye, deep earth chakras		
COLOR: Metallic gray	CLARITY: Opaque and glossy	TEMPERATURE: Cooling
PHYSICAL HEALING QUALITIES: Helps heal wounds; treats anemia and issues related to perineum; improves blood circulation; increases male potency and physical strength; place on lung to help respiration		
EMOTIONAL HEALING QUALITIES: Balancing and calming; hold to third eye for psychic and interstellar information; connects with earth, facilitating sense of security		

NUUMMITE

("SORCERER'S STONE," QUARTZ, FELDSPAR)

CHAKRA: Eighth and ninth (earth) chakras		
COLOR: Black or dark brown, sometimes with rainbow reflections	CLARITY: Opaque	TEMPERATURE: Cooling

PHYSICAL HEALING QUALITIES: Deeply grounding for immediate calming; relieves tension headaches and stress; brings vitalizing energy through foot chakras into physical body; heals feet, ankles, lower spine, and tissues; formed in volcanoes, its strong electromagnetic field brings powerful EMF and other protection

EMOTIONAL HEALING QUALITIES: Known as the "truth serum of the stone world"; helps bring subconscious to consciousness; uncovers repressed emotions for healing

BLACK OBSIDIAN

(VOLCANIC GLASS MINERALOID)

CHAKRA: Eighth and ninth chakras (in earth below feet)		
COLOR: Glossy black	CLARITY: Opaque	TEMPERATURE: Cooling

PHYSICAL HEALING QUALITIES: Energizes basic life force; releases negativity that underlies physical symptoms; shields against energy drain; eases depression; enhances self-control, relaxation, and discipline; alleviates arthritis and other inflammatory conditions

EMOTIONAL HEALING QUALITIES: Helps create psychic shield; clears negative psychic energy; instills mental and emotional positivity and stability

CHANNELED HEALING QUALITIES: Improves circulation; treats arterial hardening; treats gallbladder problems; balances digestion; reduces cravings; aids vision; works with DNA

SHUNGITE

(98 PERCENT CARBON, MINERALOID)

CHAKRAS: Lower earth chakras		
COLOR: Black	CLARITY: Opaque	TEMPERATURE: Cooling

PHYSICAL HEALING QUALITIES: Antibacterial; antifungal; antioxidant; balances and restores bioenergetic field; absorbs radiation and negative energies; protects against EMF rays; purifies water; shields from radio waves and electromagnetic disturbances; reverses physical dysfunction, tiredness, depression, and chronic illness

EMOTIONAL HEALING QUALITIES: Brings sense of well-being and positivity; balances electromagnetic field to balance, vitalize, and heal emotional and mental disturbances; either wear shungite, sweep through aura, or place near EMF or radio wave sources (NOTE: It is important to clear shungite at least once a month. Replace it every six to twelve months, as needed. To clear, place shungite in four cups of water with one tablespoon of lemon for eight hours. Then, let it sit in sun for three hours)

TEKTITE

(SILICA GLASS WITH MAGNESIUM AND IRON)

CHAKRA: Crown chakra or chakra about one to three feet above the crown; heart chakra (moldavite)

COLOR: Black, sometimes glossy; moldavite (also a tektite) is green (NOTE: These are not meteorites, but result from meteorite impact)	CLARITY: Opaque to transparent	TEMPERATURE: Cooling (black tektite); warming (moldavite)

PHYSICAL HEALING QUALITIES: Calming; black tektite brings stability

EMOTIONAL HEALING QUALITIES: Connects with universal, interplanetary energy; increases telepathy, lucid dreaming, dream recall, psychic powers, and astral travel; brings broader life perspective; moldavite helps join the heart with the expanded mind; place on crown to raise awareness of karmic potential and higher life purpose

CHANNELED HEALING QUALITIES: Speeds healing; slows aging; improves memory and mental sharpness

WHITE CORAL
(SKELETIZED ORGANIC LIVING OCEAN ORGANISMS)

CHAKRA: Crown chakra		
COLOR: White	CLARITY: Opaque	TEMPERATURE: Cooling
PHYSICAL HEALING QUALITIES: Strengthens skeletal muscle and bone, tendons, ligaments, synovial tissue, and cardiac muscle		
EMOTIONAL HEALING QUALITIES: Calming; grounds spiritual energies into body; balances earth, water, and sky elements in mind and emotions; attracts positive emotions; brings stability and confidence		
CHANNELED HEALING QUALITIES: Helps colds, bronchitis, asthma, and infections with mucus discharge; worn on navel, helps avoid miscarriage and promotes safe delivery		

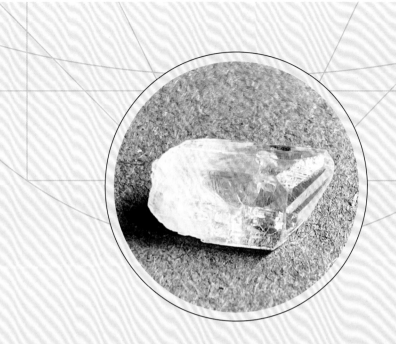

CLEAR DANBURITE

CHAKRA: Crown chakra		
COLOR: Colorless	CLARITY: Translucent or transparent	TEMPERATURE: Cooling

PHYSICAL HEALING QUALITIES: Rebalances and stimulates endocrine system, including the pineal, pituitary, and hypothalamus glands, and the brain; regulates metabolism, blood pressure, hormones, heart rate, appetite, and body temperature; treats muscular and motor problems, boosts melatonin production; treats sleep disorders and migraine headaches; eases pain and calms nervous system

EMOTIONAL HEALING QUALITIES: Brings angelic energy for harmony, creativity, optimism, and cooperation; aids relationships; connects with higher subtle bodies to relieve limiting karmic and behavioral patterns; releases anxiety and stress

HERKIMER DIAMOND
("ENLIGHTENMENT CRYSTAL")

CHAKRA: Crown, third eye, throat, and heart chakras		
COLOR: Clear	CLARITY: Transparent	TEMPERATURE: Warming or cooling (depends on intention)

PHYSICAL HEALING QUALITIES: Especially amplifying and energizing; increases ability to diagnose; stimulates subtle and physical nervous systems, fluid movement of body, and internal organ function; releases all forms of negative energy (NOTE: True Herkimer diamonds, the brightest and most powerful of all quartz crystals, are only found in Herkimer County, New York)

EMOTIONAL HEALING QUALITIES: Brings spiritual and angelic positive energy, higher consciousness, and expanded awareness; grounds what is formless into physical, mental, and emotional form; opens third eye for psychic abilities, including clairvoyance, clairaudience, and clairsentience; enhances insight, creativity, and truthfulness; alleviates fear, worry, insecurity, and feelings of worthlessness, bringing knowledge of true self and essential oneness with others and all forms of life

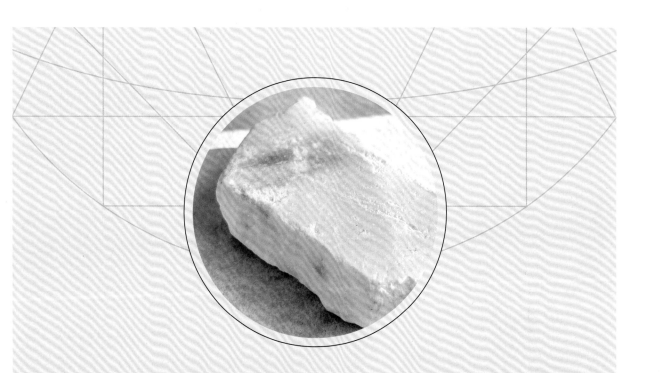

WHITE MARBLE
(CRYSTALLINE, RELATED TO CALCITE)

CHAKRA: Crown and earth chakras		
COLOR: White	CLARITY: Opaque	TEMPERATURE: Cooling

PHYSICAL HEALING QUALITIES: Purifying; soothes pain and stress; strengthens immune system; calms inflammatory blood and skin conditions; related to earth element, helps bones, teeth, hair, and nails; instills calming and stabilizing earth energy

EMOTIONAL HEALING QUALITIES: Instills serenity, inner peace, and a sense of firmness, mental steadiness, and protection; calms emotional upset and excitability; clears emotional negativity

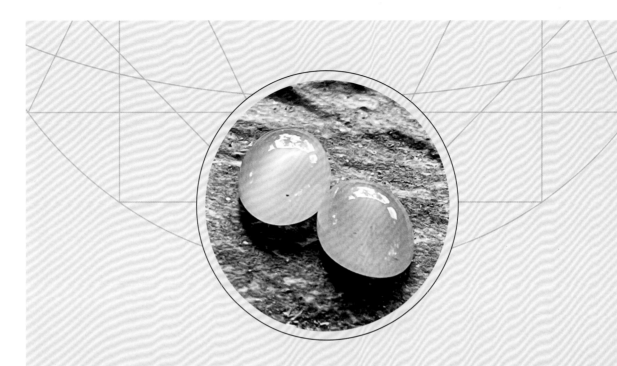

WHITE MOONSTONE
(FELDSPAR)

CHAKRA: Crown, third eye, heart, and second chakras		
COLOR: White, off-white, or cream	CLARITY: Opaque, translucent, or transparent	TEMPERATURE: Cooling

PHYSICAL HEALING QUALITIES: Related to water element; helps release all energetic blockages; regulates the flow of fluids in the body, including circulation; related to the moon's feminine energy, it helps with childbirth, pregnancy, female fertility, PMS, and sensuality

EMOTIONAL HEALING QUALITIES: Increases intuition, psychic abilities, clairvoyance, and insight; channels spiritual energy and higher consciousness of crown chakra; related to the ebb and flow of tides, it helps balance disturbed emotions, relieves stubbornness, and eases emotional rigidity; transmutes negative emotions and emotional trauma; instills deep calm and inner peace

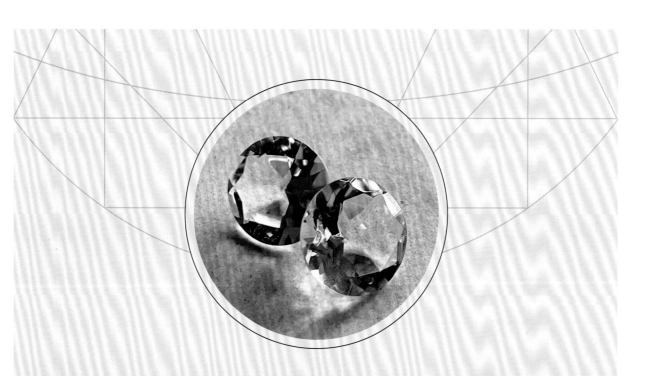

WHITE TOPAZ

CHAKRA: Third eye and crown chakras, chakras above crown		
COLOR: Colorless	CLARITY: Transparent	TEMPERATURE: Warming or cooling (depending on intention)

PHYSICAL HEALING QUALITIES: Extremely energizing; magnifies physical healing of all bodily functions and intentions; amplifies healing chakras in hand; aids diagnosis

EMOTIONAL HEALING QUALITIES: Enhances mental and emotional clarity, positivity, intuition, psychic abilities, clairsentience, clairvoyance, and lucid dreaming; helps to discern higher truth and deep truths about self and others; connects with divine will to rebalance emotions

CRYSTAL AND STONE HEALING DOESN'T REPLACE STANDARD MEDICAL CARE

Finally, it is very important to realize and communicate that your crystal healing work is meant to complement, not substitute for standard medical help or traditional diagnosis. It is not a sign of not being a good crystal healer if you encourage your clients to also consult a medical professional. It merely protects you from getting in trouble. You may want to also post a sign in your healing space or have the person you are working with sign a simple form acknowledging this. Not only that, but you, yourself, should be willing to consult a medical professional when needed.

Chapter 8
CRYSTAL HEALING TECHNIQUES

There are several techniques that you can utilize in your crystal healing practice that go beyond simply laying your crystals on the body, carrying them, or wearing them. You can combine your crystals with visualizations, mudras (yogic hand positions,) sounds, mantras, or affirmations. You can use your clear quartz crystals to *actively manipulate* subtle energy to affect the physical body, thoughts, or emotions. You can make crystal tonic water. You can perform distance healing.

The following chapter will teach you how to use multiple techniques in your healing practice.

LAYING CRYSTALS AND STONES ON THE BODY

Laying a crystal or stone on the physical body will cause the body's subtle energy to resonate with the stone's energy as the two vibrational patterns and rates begin to harmonize. Laying the crystal with a focused intention will be even more powerful. The more you focus your intention, the more potent the healing effect will be.

Besides creating a safe environment within which to do your healing, you need to center and ground yourself as suggested earlier in this book. If you are working with another person, you need to also help them be centered and grounded. This will protect you and sensitize you to the crystal energy, which will help guide your actions.

BASIC CRYSTAL HEALING PATTERN

This crystal pattern is one that you can use for any type of healing. First, place a crystal that matches the color of each chakra on that chakra point. In other words, lay a yellow crystal on the yellow third chakra, a turquoise stone on the turquoise throat chakra, and so on, until they form a rainbow of color, from the red at the bottom of the spine to the violet on the top of the crown.

I usually begin with the heart chakra, moving down to the third chakra, up to the third eye, then below the feet, and finally above the head. This balances the initial work of opening the chakras. You can fill in the rest of the crystals on each chakra in the order that seems right to you. Once you have done this, place a clear quartz crystal in each upward-facing hand. The termination should point toward the arm in the left hand and outward in the right hand. Though this pattern is powerful enough for any crystal healing, you may want to augment it with the addition of other crystals. If so, after the basic healing pattern is in place, lay crystals on any of the other energy channels that seem to need clearing, as well as on any other specific location that needs healing.

Knowing how you lay your crystals and stones on the physical body is as important as knowing where to lay them. You should not thoughtlessly place stones on the body without paying deeper attention to the process. First, you should be completely centered, grounded, and in tune with the crystals and the part of the body on which you intend to lay them. Next, begin to slowly lower the crystal to the surface of the body while remaining extremely attentive to the process. As you lower the crystal or stone, you will notice a force field between the crystal and the body. It feels somewhat like the buoyant sensation when you place your hand on top of a balloon. There is a give to the energy field, as well as a gentle solidity. When you feel this, you are physically sensing the electromagnetic field or aura of the physical body. If you don't feel this, sensitize the energy centers in the middle of your hands until you can.

Once you are in contact with the body's energy field in the place where you want to lay your crystal, you need to make sure that the body is accepting the crystal rather than repelling it. (Generally speaking, if the body seems to be repelling the crystal, it is not the right stone to place there.) If the body is accepting the crystal, you will feel a sense of give, almost like an opening or a sensation that the crystal is being drawn inward through the aura to the body beneath. If the body is not accepting the crystal, you will feel more of a resistance, as if the aura is casting the stone away from itself.

As soon as you feel the accepting sensation, slowly lower the crystal to the body while maintaining your connection to both the crystal and the accepting aura. Only then do you lay the stone completely upon the physical body. Before you pick up and lay the next crystal on the body, be sure to clear your hand. In order to remain sensitized to this process, I like to hold a clear quartz crystal in my left receiving hand and lay the stones with my imparting right hand. You can continue laying the crystals or stones on the body until you feel as if the subtle body will not receive any more. If you are paying attention, you will know when you have laid enough stones on the body.

Once the stones are in place, you can amplify their effects by using a single terminated clear quartz crystal as a wand to send the energy of the stone into the body. To do this, use your right hand to point its tip toward the colored crystal on the body. Then with focused intention, actively

visualize the energy of the clear crystal in your hand entering into the colored stone on the body. Visualize the stone's energy increasing and then powerfully entering the body. Continue to hold the other clear quartz crystal in your left hand to energize yourself and the process.

Once you have finished, clear your crystal by running it through your smudging smoke and/or touching its tip to the earth while imagining that any negative energy or color influence clears and enters the earth. Continue this process with the next crystal that you lay upon the body.

ADDING MORE CRYSTALS

Once you have placed the crystals on the body, continue to pay attention to them while tuning into the physical and subtle bodies at the same time. As you continue to focus, you might sense that one or more of the crystals wants to be replaced with another, or removed entirely, as the crystal healing progresses. That means that the crystal's job is done for now. If so, consciously remove the crystal and clear it. Then either leave its location empty or consciously place another crystal there.

It is not at all unusual to replace and move crystals as the healing progresses or your sense of what is needed deepens. For example, you may start by laying a yellow crystal on the third chakra or abdomen to bring vitality to someone who is tired all of the time. Then in a few moments you realize that the abdominal center has been activated enough. At the same time, you sense that you should put blue crystals on the lung points. As you do so, you realize that the fatigue is due to a lung problem and faulty respiration. Once you energetically activate the lungs, you may get a depressed feeling within you. Knowing that *you* aren't the one who is depressed, you realize that *the other person* is depressed. Reasoning that a lack of air has created the depression, you add an uplifting white crystal above the amethyst at the crown chakra to help alleviate the depression. To amplify the effect, you may also add white stones (or clear crystals that have been programmed with white) alongside the blue crystals on the lung points.

As you can see in the example above, placing stones on the body for a healing is usually a fluid process rather than a static one. Rarely do you lay a set of stones on the body and find that the work is done. Even in the basic crystal layout pattern, you probably will find yourself adding or subtracting crystals as your understanding of the problem develops.

There is no set amount of time that you should keep the crystals on the body, although a good healing session usually lasts anywhere from a half hour to forty-five minutes. Whether you are moving, adding, or subtracting crystals, continue until you begin to feel tired, your client gets restless, or it seems like time to stop. Then consciously remove the crystals from the body in the reverse order in which you laid them down, briefly clearing each stone in your smudging smoke after you remove it. I usually like to remove the crystal on the heart last so that the person is left in a state of love and acceptance.

When you are finished, ask the person you are working with to open their eyes. After ensuring that they are grounded, discuss your findings and explain what you did with the stones. (Sometimes I do this during the healing. If so, I use a quiet, hypnotic voice to keep them in a meditative, receptive state.)

CRYSTAL TONIC WATER

Learning to charge water with clear quartz or colored crystals will give you another useful tool in your crystal healing practice. You can do this either for an increased sense of vitality and well-being, or for healing specific types of physical, mental, and emotional problems. When you charge water, you imbue it with the energy of certain crystals, thus creating a revitalizing, healing beverage.

Use crystals that align well with the type of healing you intend to do. The energy of clear quartz, for example, acts as a general preventative measure against all types of ill health. If you want to raise your energy level, you might use clear quartz crystal or a yellow crystal, like yellow citrine. If you want to open your heart chakra, you might charge your water with rose quartz or a green serpentine jade. Amethyst is appropriate for a nonspecific healing, and black tourmaline will help you to feel protected.

In order to make a crystal or stone tonic, begin by clearing the crystal you plan to use. Once cleared, you may program it with an affirmation, a prayer, a tone, or any influence you like. Next, fill a clear glass container with distilled or pure spring water and carefully drop in your crystal. After sensitizing your hands, center your focus on the container while holding your palms facing downward about three or four inches above its top. You should feel a buoyancy between your palms and the water. With your palms still facing downward, circle your hands three or four times in a clockwise direction over the top of the container. If you are sufficiently sensitized, you will experience a change in the feeling between your palms and the crystallized water. Once this change occurs, you have created your crystal tonic; the properties of the water have been altered to match those of the crystal's energy, as well as any programming you may have done. When you drink this crystal tonic, the charged water will affect your body accordingly. It will even taste different than it did before the charging.

If you are in a hurry, you can drink some or all of the crystal tonic immediately. However, the effects of your charging will become much stronger if you place the container in sunlight for an hour, a day, or even three days. The longer you leave it in the sunlight, the stronger your charged water will be. Afterward, you can store some or all of it in your refrigerator for later use. Often, only a few restorative sips are needed at a time; in cases of acute illness, however, you might want to drink a full glass every fifteen minutes for the first hour, then smaller amounts throughout the rest of the day. Once you have finished making the tonic, be sure to clear the crystal before using it again.

You may want to charge more than one container at a time, each with a different crystal, so that you have tonics available for a variety of uses. You can also put multiple crystals in one container, combining rose quartz and amethyst, for example, for love and healing, or smoky quartz and red garnet for a grounded sense of security. (Be sure to label your containers so that you know which is which.) When you create crystal tonics for the people you are healing, you might offer them one or more containers to take with them and sip from over the next few days.

DISTANCE HEALING

As long as you are able to focus one-pointedly, distance healing can be as effective as healing in person. Just as in traditional healing, be sure to get the person's permission before you start—unless, of course, you are sending healing that is universally good for everyone, such as general health, calmness of spirit, love, and joy.

One way to perform distance healing is to visualize the other person very clearly in your mind's eye, then use your single terminated clear crystal "wand" to send them the healing energy they need. This process requires that you either see the person as if the healing has already happened or envision the healing energy as it enters them and makes the desired changes. You can strengthen the healing by holding either an amethyst or energizing clear crystal in your left hand as you send out the energy with your right.

Another effective method begins with making an altar or undisturbed special place and positioning the person's picture in the middle of it. Once this is done, place a small paper describing the healing you would like to occur directly under the picture, then surround the picture and paper with the appropriate healing crystals. If the crystals have points or terminations, direct them in toward the picture. Next, surround these crystals with single terminated clear quartz crystals, tips inward, for further energy. Use the size that seems appropriate to you; however, the clear quartz crystals should not be larger than the other healing crystals. Place lighted candles on each side of the crystal formation and picture, making sure that the flames are far enough away and won't set the picture on fire. Finally, holding a double terminated clear crystal, amethyst, or Herkimer diamond in each hand, visualize sending healing energy to the person in the picture. You can also send accompanying prayers or healing affirmations.

When you are finished, you can let the candles burn for as long as safety allows. You might keep them lit until they completely burn down, then replace them. Some people keep the candles going overnight, while others don't feel this is safe.

You can either remove the altar after the first distance-healing session or leave it up for as long as you like. To dismantle the altar, begin by removing the crystals and candles. Then remove the paper with the healing description and burn it completely (and safely), imagining the smoke sending healing prayers and intentions to the higher spirit. Once you have completed this step, reverently remove the picture and put it wherever you feel is best, then clear all of the crystals.

VISUALIZATION

Our sense of reality is totally dependent on the mind. That can be understood in two ways: The first is the spiritual interpretation—that the mind creates shape and form, endings and beginnings for what is essentially endless and formless, including our own bodies. It is our ego-self that embraces our individual identity based on our thoughts, feelings, and the appearance of our physical body.

The second interpretation is that thought determines our world because it creates our experience of reality. Our thoughts, desires, and expectations form a screen through which we selectively interpret and understand "reality." How many times, for example, have we seen something one way only to find that it is something else entirely when we observe it more closely? The usual example is the snake in the road story: We think that that we see a snake in the road and react with fear, but when we look again, we realize that it is a rope, and we feel relief. Our feelings and reactions were real, but they were based on a faulty perception. As soon as our perception changed, our feelings, thoughts, and actions changed.

This dynamic permeates our physical, mental, and emotional world, not only limiting and changing our experience but also perpetuating our faulty perception. For example, if we think that a tree is green and brown, we will see it that way and fail to notice the additional orange leaves that have turned color or the streaks of black in the trunk. Similarly, if we think that people don't like us, we will primarily notice what seems to be evidence of their dislike and disregard any observations that contradict that thought. Likewise, if we think we are suffering from a specific illness, we will only notice symptoms of that illness, which in turn will worsen our experience of it.

These two interpretations explain why visualization works and how powerful it can be. When you use visualization to influence a thought (and associated feelings), you shift the way in which that thought constitutes your reality. The strength of your focus determines how much you are able to shift your perceptions. The more willpower you can use to strengthen your focus, the more change you can facilitate.

There is very little difference between imagination and visualization because both rely on the creative part of your mind. In fact, the brain is just as influenced by something real as by something visualized, not knowing the difference between the two. Another way to understand visualization, then, is as ultrafocused imagination.

Often during visualizations, I use the terms *imagination* and *visualization* interchangeably, not only because they are so similar but also because people often feel more comfortable with the term *imagination*. If I am leading a visualization and someone insists that they "can't visualize" or "don't see anything," I overcome this barrier by suggesting that they *imagine* seeing the visualization.

Combining visualization with crystal work enhances the potency of the healing. During a crystal healing session, I may suggest that a person visualize the crystal energy entering a particular area of the body and making positive changes. Similarly, if I determine that a particular emotional imbalance is feeding and perpetuating an illness, I may have the subject visualize a different emotion than the one they are experiencing. For example, if a person is having digestive problems and I sense that a persistent state of repressed anger is behind it, I may have them visualize their anger dissipating and being replaced with joy. Suggesting that they *visualize* joy during the healing session may help soften any resistance they have to *feeling* joy.

Just as thought empowers emotion, emotion empowers thought. Adding emotion to visualization will increase its effectiveness, especially if you use emotion to shift the negative thinking that supports the energetic imbalance behind an illness.

To do this, first picture the visualization in your mind's eye, then suggest a particular feeling to accompany it. A good way to do this is to consider positive affirmations that negate or replace the negative thought patterns. If a persistent sore throat is supported by unexpressed communications, for example, you might use the affirmation, "I feel safe to express myself," as you place turquoise on the throat chakra.

Though the effects of visualization can be wide ranging, the instructions are quite easy. You close your eyes, center and ground yourself, and focus your attention upon a specific topic or image that will be helpful for the healing. If your mind wanders, gently bring it back to the visualization. Continue doing so until you feel that it is time to stop or that your objective has been achieved. The procedure is the same whether you are doing your own visualization or guiding someone else.

To help empower visualization, you can focus on your third eye as you visualize. You can also hold clear quartz crystals in each hand. Gyan Mudra, touching the first finger to the thumb, is an excellent hand position to use because it opens the higher energy centers from which visualization manifests. You can place a small clear quartz crystal on each palm while you hold this hand position. You can also stimulate the third eye with a Herkimer diamond, lapis, sodalite, azurite, or any other royal blue crystal. You can enhance that effect by adding orange carnelian, orange calcite, or any other orange crystal in order to open your manifesting and creative second chakra.

Give yourself permission to be creative in your visualization imagery. You can visualize color, landscapes, the healing as it is happening, energy moving within your body, encountering specific healing guides, and more. You can imagine smell, touch, sound, and any other sensation. You can visualize certain feelings entering or leaving your body. There are no limits, so let your imagination guide you.

ACTIVE CRYSTAL ENERGY MANIPULATION FOR HEALING

Another effective healing technique involves using a crystal to create a balance within the subtle body so that healing can occur naturally. To do so, you actively manipulate subtle energy with your crystal in order to balance each of the chakras and energy centers with each other. This subtle energy realignment creates a corresponding change in the physical body.

There are several methods for manipulating subtle energy. You can use a single terminated crystal as a wand to direct and move energy throughout the body. Sweeping the crystal from toe to head will lift energy that is too depressed or too centered in the lower chakras and bring a portion of it into the upper chakras. Likewise, you can move energy that is too centered in the upper chakras and bring a share of it into the lower chakras. You can use your single terminated crystal wand to open blocked energy centers or close centers that are too open. If you sense a blockage, you can use your crystal to remove it. If there is an area that is overstimulated, you can use your crystal to draw out the excess energy.

You can also use a crystal like a subtle-energy "surgical knife" to cut through the unwanted energy cords of thoughts or emotions that are causing you harm. Similarly, you can use it to energetically cut through or cut out illness or disease that feels like a lump (usually gray) or a parasitic growth within the subtle body. Tumors and other physical growths can be treated by cutting out their subtle counterparts. You can use your crystal to cut through emotions that are stuck within the emotional subtle body, especially those that are supporting illness or imbalance. Similarly, you can cut through repetitive harmful thought patterns that create negative realities. Basically, anything that attaches or adheres to the subtle body on any level can be cut out of it.

You can also remove pain by sensing where it is in the physical, mental, or emotional body and then cutting it out, discarding it and replacing it with its opposite. It is important that you discard what was removed into the earth, actually visualizing it entering into the ground and seeing it transmuted into positivity and healing energy.

When you energetically cut something out of the subtle body with your crystal, you leave behind a hole that needs filling. Generally, you want to fill the hole with energy that is the opposite of what you removed. You can use your wand to visualize what that energy would be and then actively send it into the body with your single terminated crystal. You can also place an appropriate crystal or stone on the physical body, right on top of the affected area, to fill it with energy.

It is usually best to use a natural clear quartz crystal to manipulate energy in these ways because, unlike a colored crystal, its versatility is not limited by color. (Of course, if you want to perform a specific task that requires a particular color, you can use the appropriate colored crystal.) Not only is a natural quartz crystal the most versatile for manipulating subtle energy, it is also generally the strongest because its original spiral formation facilitates the outward energy flow in ways that other forms of crystal do not. A single terminated quartz crystal channels the flow in one direction. If you use a double terminated crystal, you will have to expend great mental power to overcome its two-way energy flow. This can be done in a pinch, but it is very difficult to ensure the same effectiveness. Twin crystals or clusters, of course, won't work because their energy flows outward in several directions. Even if a twin crystal formed side by side so that the energy flow is in alignment, the force of the flow will be somewhat dissipated or split. If you use a quartz crystal that has been cut and polished, make sure it was carved in alignment with the natural energy flow of the stone, or its efficacy will be compromised.

To direct energy outward from a single terminated clear quartz crystal, you merely have to point it outward and imagine the energy flowing in that direction. The stronger your focus, the more powerful the energy flow will be. If you are shifting or removing energy in any way, you should also couple your focused attention with the gestures and movements of your crystal.

To lift energy in the subtle body, point your crystal to the bottom of the spine or the feet and slowly move it up the body, visualizing the subtle energy following its path. To move energy downward, do the opposite, starting at the top of the crown. If you want to channel earth energy upward into the body, point the crystal to the earth below the feet, visualize the energy entering your crystal, and move your crystal upward. Likewise, if you want to channel energy from the higher planes into the subtle body, point the tip of the crystal a few inches to two or three feet above the center of the head, visualize the energy entering into your crystal, and then move the crystal from head to toe.

To remove energy from the subtle body, point your crystal at the affected area and spiral it in smaller and smaller circles until you reach the area's center, continuing to focus with unwavering attention. When you reach the center, "hook" the energy and figuratively pull it out. You will know you have hooked it when you feel a slight energetic pull or tug. Once you have pulled the energy out, send it into the earth. You may find that you need to hook and pull more than once. Stop once you no longer feel anything left to hook, or once you have a definite sense that you have done enough.

You also can send energy and intentions into the subtle body to create balance. First, identify and visualize what is needed, then point your crystal toward it, hook it, and imagine it entering the crystal. Transfer it to the body by pointing the crystal and visualizing the energy entering the body. Continue until you feel a definite sense that you have done enough.

Once you are finished, use your awareness to perform a complete scan of the subtle body and see if it now feels balanced. If not, continue working until you sense a balance. Then, use a double terminated crystal to smooth the aura or subtle energy field around the physical body, locking in the changes you have made as you imagine the subtle energy field being cleared. (You can use the same single terminated crystal to do this by holding it sideways after you have cleared it.) Next, lay down all of your crystals and clear them. Perform a finishing clearing by smudging yourself, the other person, and the surrounding environment.

Lastly, to increase your subtle awareness and to empower both your personal energy and the crystal you are using, hold a double terminated crystal in your left hand. Visualize that this charging crystal, connected with the one in your right hand, is bringing energy and information into you.

Chapter 9
CRYSTAL HEALING FOR COMMON PHYSICAL AILMENTS

The next two chapters cover specific crystal healing techniques to get you started. From these you will be able to extrapolate other techniques that work with other ailments. Ultimately, of course, you will want to be able to sense which crystals and which techniques are best suited to the treatment of a particular condition.

When addressing these healing techniques, I have used many of the colored crystals and stones from both the primary and secondary crystal healing kits. There are a few general steps to take before you begin using a specific technique. First, lay the stones where I suggest, then use your two clear crystals to scan the subtle body for any other areas that seem connected with the physical, mental, or emotional ailments that you are healing. Once you have found these areas, use your clear crystals, as illustrated earlier, to remove, cut through, send in, or otherwise manipulate the subtle energy to complete the preliminary healing. You should continue this crystal healing process until it seems like time to stop. Then you are ready to begin using a specific technique.

Once again, it is important that you or the person you are working with consult the appropriate medical professional, whether a Western or Eastern osteopathic doctor or allopathic physician. The work that you do will complement their techniques. Do not tell someone to avoid taking medicine prescribed by a professional. You can give a second opinion based on any subtle components you see, but make sure the person you are healing understands that your insights represent an *opinion*, no matter how versed you are in subtle energy crystal work. Of course, if someone chooses not to take the advice or prescribed medicine offered by a medical professional, that is certainly their prerogative. Just make sure that it really is *their* choice and not *yours*. This advice is not meant as a comment on your skill; rather, it is intended to keep you safe from lawsuits. And, of course, it is always good to realize that you may not be right in every case.

A LITTLE HUMILITY GOES A LONG WAY TOWARD BUILDING YOUR SKILL INSTEAD OF YOUR EGO.

When crystal healing, it is important to realize that rarely, if ever, do physical illnesses and diseases occur without a mental or emotional component. Usually, the physical, mental, and emotional imbalances are completely intertwined, so it is important to address the complete picture every time you perform a healing. Address the more overt manifestation of the problem first, then work on the deeper layers as they become exposed.

It works well to guide someone in a short relaxation technique before you begin. This moves the mind into a lightly altered state and relaxes the body so that crystal healing can be effective.

Here, then, are some physical crystal healing techniques to get you started. If you don't have one or more of the stones mentioned, remember that you can always use a programmed clear quartz.

BONE FRACTURE AND COMPOUND FRACTURE

1. Lightly rub a white howlite or white calcite on the fracture, then set it down directly on top of the injured area (make sure it is not heavy). If the fracture is large, place more than one howlite or calcite on the entire area.

2. Surround the fracture with green calcite to cool the heat and pain. Alternate with green chrysocolla (for its copper content) to help heal the bones and skin.

3. Place a smoky quartz below each foot to draw out pain while drawing in earth energy for bone and skin healing.

4. Surround the body with four or eight amethysts to heal the fracture and the wound, and to relieve shock to the subtle and physical systems.

5. Use a clear quartz crystal to visualize knitting the bones together and to pull out the pain.

6. Drink tonic water made with white howlite, chrysocolla, and amethyst.

SPRAINS (TORN LIGAMENTS)

1. Lightly rub a red hematite crystal over the torn ligament, then place it on top of the ligament for tissue regeneration and healing earth energy.

2. Surround the tear with green tourmaline to minimize trauma, relieve pain, and calm inflammation.

3. Place smoky quartz crystals under the feet to draw on earth energy.

4. Surround the body with selenite for calming.

5. Trace the ligament in the subtle body with a single terminated quartz crystal while visualizing the injured area repairing itself.

6. Drink tonic water made of green tourmaline, amethyst, and smoky quartz.

FLU

1. Place a soothing yellow amber on the navel point, then surround this crystal with four hematite crystals to relieve nausea, and boost the immune system.

2. Place a blue lace agate over each lung to help with breathing.

3. Place a very warm cloth or washrag over the forehead, eyes, and sinuses. Set an amethyst on each side of the head, and a blue/green/violet fluorite in the middle of the forehead to help relieve congestion and headache.

4. Place an amethyst at the base of the skull to further relieve headache.

5. Place a black tourmaline about six inches below the feet. Visualize the black crystal drawing all toxins into the core of the earth while channeling healing earth energies back into the subtle and physical bodies.

6. Hold a brown crystal in each hand to further absorb pain, bring calm, and channel healing earth energy.

7. Surround the body with eight clear quartz crystals, their tips pointing away from the body. Visualize these crystals connecting to each other, surrounding the body with a cooling, nurturing, light green healing aura.

8. Drink tonic water made with clear quartz crystal and amber.

COLDS

1. Place a yellow citrine over the solar plexus to boost the immune system and vitalize the subtle and physical bodies.

2. Place a turquoise on the throat chakra to help relieve coughing and relax the muscles of the throat.

3. Place a hematite in the middle of the chest to open the lungs.

4. Place a blue lace agate on each side of the forehead to help open the sinuses.

5. Place a black crystal below the feet to draw out toxins.

6. Periodically breathe in the steam of quartz crystal water to open the sinuses and bring vital, healing energy.

7. Drink tonic water made of amber and quartz crystal.

CANCER

There are many types of cancer, so use crystals that will work with the affected parts of the body: white howlite with bones, blue lapis with the brain, yellow citrine with the stomach, and so on. In addition, the amethyst crystal formation described here will work with any type of cancer.

1. Place a double terminated clear quartz crystal or Herkimer diamond about six inches above the top of the head. Place a black agate, tourmaline, or onyx below the feet, its tip pointed downward if terminated. Visualize a bright, clear, angelic healing energy flowing down from the quartz into the crown and on through the body; picture this energy as a stream of cleansing and energizing light. Imagine it drawing out toxins as it flows down through the black stone into the earth.

2. Next, place a rose quartz crystal on the heart chakra as you imagine it blossoming into a beautiful and loving rose. Breathe in its infinite love and total acceptance. Do this for at least three minutes.

3. Now place an amethyst on the third chakra, on the solar plexus. Place additional amethysts on the throat chakra, the second chakra, the third eye, the first chakra, and the crown chakra. Imagine these stones filling the entire body with healing, angelic, calming violet light. Imagine this light extending outward about three feet to surround the body.

4. Hold an amethyst crystal in each hand, pointing the tips upward if terminated, and imagine that their violet light flows up into the body.

5. Use a single terminated clear quartz crystal to pull out and release any areas that seem blocked, irritated, hot, excessively cold, or otherwise indicative of the negative energy associated with cancer symptoms, including any related negative emotional or thought patterns. (If working on yourself, do this before you place the crystals on the body.)

6. Drink tonic water made with clear quartz and amethyst crystals.

HEALING THE EYES
(EYE STRAIN OR DISEASE)

1. Close the eyes. Place a blue azurite or lapis on the third eye point. Then place a green aventurine or small green malachite cabochon or crystal on each eyelid.

2. Surround the eyes with six small yellow citrine or bright yellow jade cabochons or crystals—one above and below each eye, and another to their sides.

3. Place an amethyst beside or behind each ear, their tips, if terminated, pointing in toward the face. Place another above the crown chakra with the tip pointing downward if terminated. Place a small turquoise or pale blue crystal on the throat chakra.

4. Place another small tumbled or smoothed amethyst behind the neck at the base of the skull.

5. Place a light green calcite, fluorite, or jade on the heart chakra.

6. Hold a clear quartz crystal in each hand to help amplify the energy of this healing.

7. Take long, deep breaths, relaxing any tension in the face, eyes, ears, skull, throat, and body with every exhale. With every inhale, imagine green light travelling in through the heart chakra and up to the eyes. Relax the eyes.

8. Drink tonic water made with a royal blue azurite, green malachite or jade, yellow jade or citrine, and amethyst.

HEADACHES

Headaches can result from tension, muscle strain, eye strain, and emotional anxiety Eliminating tension or anxiety will usually help relieve symptoms. **NOTE:** Thunderclap headaches that develop in sixty seconds or less are the result of a brain hemorrhage, stroke, or brain aneurysm. CALL 911 IMMEDIATELY.

1. Surround the body with amethyst crystals. If terminated, the tips should point away from the body. Energetically connect the amethysts with a clear crystal to create a violet, energetic aura around the body.

2. Place a smoky quartz below and touching the center arch of each foot. If terminated, point the tips away from the body.

3. Place a sizeable black tourmaline or other black stone about eight inches to a foot below each smoky quartz, anchoring the subtle body energy deep into the earth.

4. Hold a smoky quartz or other brown stone in each hand. If terminated, point the tips toward the earth.

5. Place a rose quartz, pink tourmaline, or other pink crystal on the heart chakra in the middle of the chest.

6. Next, place a green crystal in the middle of the belly and an amethyst on each side of the waist. If they are terminated, point the tips toward the earth.

7. Place an amethyst crystal on each side of the head behind the ears. If terminated, point the tips away from the head, parallel to the earth.

8. Once these crystals are in place, breathe in amethyst and release tension with every exhale.

9. Once you are relaxed, place a blue celestite or other pale blue crystal in the center of the forehead and on each cheekbone. Surround the celestite with pale green jades or other pale green crystals.

10. Visualize the forehead opening like the sky until it is filled with gentle, blue space. Have the person drink amethyst and blue lace agate tonic water.

MIGRAINES

1. Migraines can be caused by emotional anxiety, contraceptives, alcohol (especially red wine), chocolate, food additives, lack of sleep, or hormonal changes. When healing, these causes should be investigated and, if possible, eliminated.

2. Surround the body with amethysts, tips pointing away from the body if terminated, and use a clear quartz crystal to connect them in a surrounding violet aura.

3. Place a smoky quartz or other brown crystal below the arch of each foot, tips pointing downward if terminated. Hold a brown crystal in each hand, tips pointing toward the earth if terminated.

4. Place a black tourmaline eight inches to a foot below the smoky quartz for detox and deep grounding.

5. Place a rose quartz on the heart chakra and a lepidolite on the belly to combat nausea and induce deep calm.

6. Place a celestite or blue quartz in the middle of the forehead and a small black cabochon crystal on each closed eye. Place another pale blue stone on the side of the head that is most in pain.

7. Hold an amethyst in each hand. Relax with every breath.

8. Drink tonic water made with amethyst, smoky quartz, and a pale blue crystal.

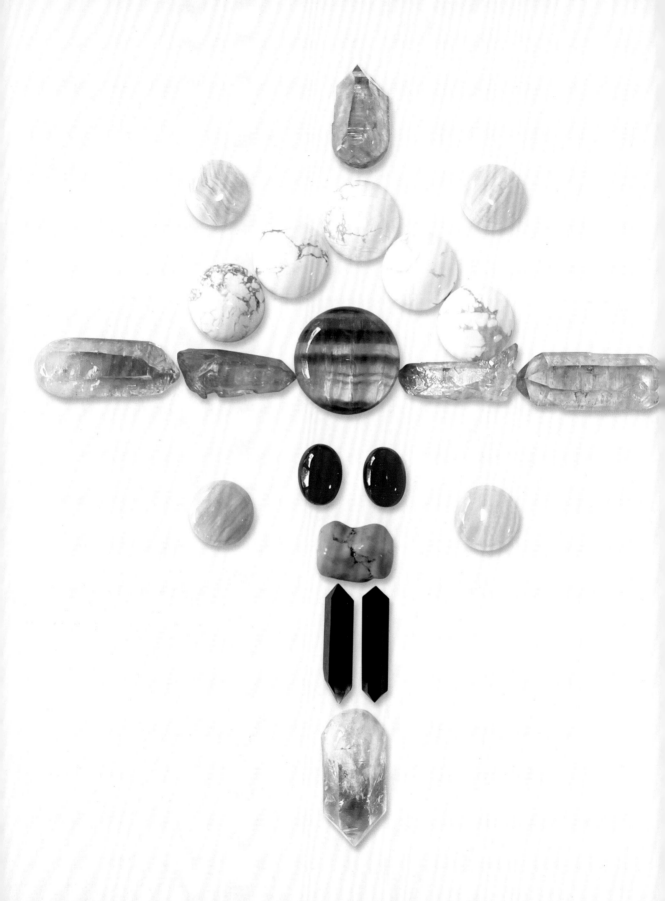

SINUS INFECTION OR ALLERGIES

1. Surround the body with alternating amethyst and blue lace agate crystals.

2. Place a green/purple/blue fluorite in the middle of the forehead. Place a small blue lace agate, celestite, or other pale blue crystal on each side of the fluorite near the temples.

3. Place a small carnelian under the eyes on each cheek to help draw out infection.

4. Place a turquoise or turquoise-colored crystal on the throat chakra.

5. Surround the entire head with white howlite, marble, or other opaque white stones. If terminated, point the tips away from the head.

6. Place a brown aragonite, smoky quartz, or any other brown crystal below the arch of each foot, tips pointing downward.

7. Drink tonic water made with white marble, amethyst, and carnelian.

NERVOUS SYSTEM
OR NERVE DISORDERS

1. Surround the body with quartz crystals: one above the head, another below the feet, and one, two, or three evenly spaced at each side. In between each crystal, place a yellow tiger eye. This will calm the nervous system. Use a clear quartz to connect these stones in an energizing yellow aura.

2. Place a yellow citrine on the abdominal third chakra. Place another yellow citrine on the actual navel point. Hold a yellow crystal in each hand, the tips pointing away from the hand if single terminated.

3. Place an orange aventurine or carnelian about three inches below the belly button.

4. Place a red garnet or other red crystal at the bottom of the spine.

5. Place a fluorite in the center of the forehead.

6. Place white howlite or marble on each side of the head above the ears.

7. Put two smoky quartz crystals or two brown stones below the center arch of each foot.

8. Use a single terminated clear quartz crystal to energize each stone and draw any overexcitement or blockages down through the body and out of the crystals below each foot. Especially energize the yellow crystals.

9. Drink tonic water made of yellow and clear quartz crystals.

EXHAUSTION (ADRENAL FATIGUE)

1. Surround the body with alternating amethyst and green calcite, green fluorite, green tourmaline, or other green crystals.

2. Place a brown aragonite, smoky quartz, or other brown crystal below the center arch of each foot. Place a black tourmaline or other black stone about eight inches to a foot below the brown crystals. Keep the black stone's tip pointing upward toward the body, allowing it to draw in strong, vitalizing earth energies.

3. Place a bright yellow calcite, citrine, or other yellow crystal about three inches above the belly button. Place another yellow crystal directly on the belly button. Connect the two with smaller, double terminated quartz crystals. Place a yellow citrine or yellow tiger eye slightly above each hip bone, keeping them in line with the center abdominal crystal. This will simultaneously energize and relax the adrenal glands.

4. Place a green tourmaline on the heart chakra and breathe in the green energy of this crystal with long, deep, relaxed breaths.

5. Next, place an orange carnelian or other orange crystal near the second chakra, just above the pubic bone. Now relax.

6. Drink tonic water made from yellow citrine, orange carnelian, green aventurine, and clear quartz.

HEART HEALTH

1. Place a pink kunzite, pink tourmaline, or rose quartz on the heart chakra.

2. Surround the pink crystal with four chrysocolla or green tourmaline stones—one above, one below, and one at each side. If the crystals are terminated, point the tips outward.

3. Hold a green tourmaline, chrysocolla, or other green crystal in each hand, tips pointing up toward the arms if terminated.

4. Place a white howlite, white marble, or white moonstone just below the throat on the upper chest. Place another on the abdomen, one more on the right side of the green crystal to the right of the center pink stone, and another on the left side of the crystal to the left of the pink center stone. You have basically made a cross pattern with the pink stone in the center.

5. Place a red garnet or jasper at the base of the spine and a red hematite between the feet.

6. Surround the body with four or eight clear quartz crystals, their tips pointing inward toward the body. Visualize these crystals connecting to form an aura of energizing yet comforting light around the body.

7. Use your clear quartz crystal to move the heart energy as needed, either to pull out obstruction or send in energy.

8. Drink tonic water made from green tourmaline or another green crystal, pink kunzite or another pink crystal, and clear quartz. Program the crystals with heart healing.

CIRCULATION AND BLOOD PRESSURE

Circulation and high blood pressure are linked with not only the heart but also nerve disorders, a hypoactive thyroid, anxiety, and lung or breathing problems like asthma, bronchitis, and emphysema. Circulation and high blood pressure may also be linked to deep vein thrombosis (blood clots). *Blood clots can travel to the heart or lungs, so it is imperative that you see a medical professional immediately if you notice discoloration of the legs.*

1. Surround the body, at a distance of about twelve inches, with amethyst crystals, tips pointing toward the body if they are terminated.

2. Hold an amethyst in each hand, tips pointed toward the arms if they are terminated.

3. Place a smoky quartz or other brown stone below the center arch of each foot.

4. Place a black tourmaline or other black stone between and about six inches below the feet. If terminated, point the tip toward the earth.

5. Place a pink kunzite or rose quartz on the heart center. Surround it with four chrysocolla stones.

6. Place a small turquoise or turquoise-colored crystal on the throat chakra.

7. Lay a blue lace agate, celestite, or other light blue stone on each lung point (these are located to the sides of the heart chakra, about three inches down from the shoulder sockets).

8. Place a red agate, red hematite, red jasper, or other opaque red stone at the bottom of the spine.

9. Place small, double terminated crystals between the stones on the lung points and the heart, and between the throat and the heart. Place one double terminated crystal on each forearm and lower arm, three between the heart and the red crystal, and one on each upper and lower leg. Visualize a stream of powerful, clear, energizing light connecting each crystal along these pathways.

10. Find any blockages or obstructions by using a single terminated clear crystal to trace each pathway. Use the same crystal to draw blockages and obstructions away from the heart and lungs and out through the bottoms of the feet.

11. Drink tonic water made from smoky quartz, amethyst, and green tourmaline or another green crystal. Relax your body as you drink.

THYROID AND METABOLISM

The thyroid gland is responsible for regulating metabolism. It can either be hyperactive (overactive) or hypoactive (underactive.) If underactive, your metabolism will be lower. If overactive, your metabolism will be higher. Part of the glandular system, the thyroid is involved in a circular feedback loop between the pituitary gland and the hypothalamus, both located near the base of your brain. Treating the thyroid should also involve treatment of all of these glands, vitalizing and balancing them with each other so that they can do their work.

1. Place a turquoise or turquoise-colored crystal on the throat chakra.

2. Place a royal blue azurite, lapis, or other royal blue crystal on the third eye chakra.

3. Place another two royal blue crystals at the base of the skull, one on the right side of the spinal cord, and the other on the left side of the spinal cord.

4. Place two amber stones about three inches below the belly button, one three inches inward from the right hip bone, and the other three inches inward from the left hip bone.

5. Hold a turquoise stone in each hand.

6. Place an amethyst above the head, and a smoky quartz or other brown stone about four to six inches below the feet, equally centered between them.

7. Use your clear quartz crystal to either energize or reduce the energy of the thyroid in the center of the throat.

GLANDULAR HEALTH AND HORMONAL BALANCE

The glandular system, also called the endocrine system, and the nervous system are interconnected, one affecting the other. Very basically, the hypothalamus ("master control center") receives messages from the nerves, which then communicate to the pituitary gland. The pituitary ("master gland") regulates the other glands through the release of hormones. The glands of the endocrine system include the pituitary, thyroid, parathyroid, thymus, sex (ovaries and testes), pancreas, hypothalamus, and adrenal glands. They control growth, basic drives, and emotions of the body, body temperature, sexual identity, tissue repair, and energy generation. The following crystal pattern will help balance and energize all of the glands.

1. Surround the body with alternating smoky quartz and amethyst crystals, including an amethyst above the crown and a smoky quartz below the feet. The crystals on each side of the body should be parallel with each other. If terminated, point them inward toward the body. The bottom smoky quartz, however, should be pointing downward from the body. This creates a calming and healing aura.

2. Place a royal blue lapis or other royal blue crystal on the third eye chakra for the pituitary gland.

3. Place a turquoise or turquoise-colored crystal on the throat chakra for the thyroid and parathyroid.

4. Place one yellow citrine or other yellow crystal on the abdomen and another on top of the belly button for the adrenals and pancreas.

5. Women: Address the ovaries by placing two orange ambers or other orange crystals about three inches below the belly button, five inches apart.

6. Men: Place a red garnet or other red stone at the base of the spine for the prostate/testes.

7. Hold an amethyst in each hand.

8. Use your single terminated clear crystal to create a balance between the glands, either stimulating or reducing the amount of energy in each one.

9. Relax the body and mind as you take long, deep, gentle breaths.

LUNGS

1. Surround the body with eight evenly spaced clear quartz crystals, their tips pointing away from body, with one positioned above the head and another below the feet. Visualize these crystals creating an energy field that extends around and within the body.

2. Place a rose quartz on the heart chakra.

3. Place two blue kunzites, blue lace agates, or other pale blue crystals on each lung point (located two to three inches above and to the sides of the heart chakra). To amplify their effects, surround each of these pale blue crystals with four clear quartz crystals.

4. Place a hematite in the center of the sternum, between the pale blue and clear crystals.

5. Hold an amethyst in each hand, tips pointing inward if they are terminated.

6. Take long, deep, breaths, imagining the pale blue entering the lungs on the inhale, and all lung obstruction leaving through the feet and entering the earth on the exhale.

7. Drink tonic water made with a pale blue crystal, an amethyst, and a clear quartz.

KIDNEYS

This crystal healing pattern works to stimulate kidney function. Because high blood pressure will negatively affect your kidneys, you might want to use your stones to lower it at the same time. Working with blood healing will also be helpful because the kidneys filter your blood.

1. Surround the body with orange carnelian or clear quartz crystals that have been programmed to be orange. Use your single terminated clear crystal to energetically connect these crystals to form an orange aura around and within the body.

2. Place an orange carnelian, orange aventurine, or other orange crystal on each of the kidneys, which are situated below the ribs and on either side of the spine. You can work with the front or back of the body.

3. Lay a yellow citrine, yellow aragonite, yellow apatite, or other yellow crystal on the third chakra in the center of the abdomen.

4. Next, place a black tourmaline, onyx, or black agate about six inches below the feet to help drain any toxins into the earth.

5. Use your clear quartz crystal to circle and stimulate each orange crystal and remove any blockages that you sense. Then, stimulate the yellow stone with your crystal as you take long, deep breaths, imagining them flowing in and out of the third chakra.

6. Drink tonic water with orange carnelian or another orange crystal, yellow citrine or other yellow crystal, and clear quartz.

LIVER, SPLEEN, AND GALLBLADDER

NOTE: It is important to work with a medical professional when treating hepatitis C, cirrhosis of the liver, or infections in the liver, spleen, or gallbladder, especially if the organs are swollen.

The following crystal layout will stimulate the digestive and blood filtering functions of all three organs.

1. Surround the body with orange carnelian or clear quartz crystals that have been programmed to be orange. Use your single terminated clear crystal to energetically connect these crystals to form an orange aura around and within the body.

2. Place an orange carnelian on each side of the lower rib cage. (The spleen is to the left side of the belly under the rib cage, and the liver is to the right of the spleen.)

3. Next, place a rose quartz, pink kunzite, or another pink crystal on the heart chakra.

4. Lay one or two small double terminated clear quartz crystals to energetically connect the pink stone on the heart chakra to both of the orange crystals on the rib cage.

5. Use two more double terminated clear quartz crystals to connect the two orange crystals, making a triangle shape.

6. Place a yellow apatite, yellow aragonite, or another yellow crystal on the third chakra on the abdomen. Then, place another yellow crystal directly on the belly button. Use one or two double terminated quartz crystals to connect the yellow abdominal crystal with the crystal on the heart chakra.

7. Set a black tourmaline or other black crystal about eight to twelve inches below the feet. Point the tip downward if the crystal is terminated.

8. Use a single terminated clear quartz crystal to trace these energy pathways, charging the crystals to improve the function of the organs. Then, trace an energy pathway from the organs to the black stone while you visualize drawing out and releasing any toxins in these organs. If you feel blockages, use the clear quartz crystal to remove them, tracing a pathway down to the black stone and out into the earth.

9. Drink tonic water with orange carnelian or another orange crystal, a yellow crystal, and clear quartz.

STOMACH AND BOWELS

1. Surround the body with amethyst crystals, tips inward. Place one above the head, another below the feet, and evenly space one to three crystals on each side of the body.

2. Place a brown stone or smoky quartz crystal below the center arch of each foot.

3. Next, lay a yellow calcite or other yellow crystal directly on the navel point (belly button). Place two more yellow calcites on the body, setting one about two inches above the navel point and the other about two inches below the navel point.

4. Place an orange carnelian or other orange crystal on the belly, one to two inches above the pubic bone. If you feel that the bowels need additional soothing energy, use an orange-toned amber.

5. Hold a yellow calcite in each hand. If terminated, point the tips up toward the arms to send energy into the body.

6. Use a single terminated clear quartz crystal to spiral around the navel point, starting at the center yellow crystal and spiraling outward. If you feel any blockages in the intestinal tract or stomach, use the clear quartz crystal to pull them out and release them down the body, through the brown stones at the feet and into the earth. You can also place an amethyst or a small yellow crystal right on the blocked area to facilitate this process.

7. Drink tonic water with a yellow, orange, and brown crystals.

BRAIN FUNCTION

NOTE: IF YOU OR THE PERSON YOU ARE HEALING IS HAVING A STROKE, CALL 911 IMMEDIATELY. Symptoms of a stroke include the following:

- slurred speech
- sudden weakness and numbness of the face, leg, or arm
- blurred vision
- loss of balance or loss of bodily control
- dizziness
- severe headache
- trouble understanding and interpreting information, difficulty making decisions

The following powerful crystal healing helps balance the two sides of the brain for better mental processing and decision making. It also facilitates the building of neural connections to improve overall brain function. Additionally, you can use this crystal healing practice to bring higher awareness into mental consciousness.

1. Surround the body with clear quartz crystals and visualize an enveloping aura of strong, bright light and energy.

2. Center a black tourmaline or another black crystal about six inches below the feet but within the surrounding aura of clear crystals. (The stronger the grounding, the more you be able to open the crown chakra.)

3. Place an amethyst above the crown chakra, within the clear quartz crystal aura. Point the tip upward if it is single terminated.

4. Lay an iolite, blue lapis, or blue azurite on the third eye.

5. Place an iolite, blue lapis, or blue azurite on each side of the temple, about one inch inward and upward from the ear.

6. Set a rose quartz on the heart chakra to balance the mental energy.

7. Next, place a 1- to 1½-inch-long double terminated clear quartz crystal on the forehead, energetically connecting the third eye crystal with the amethyst on the crown.

8. Then, place two 1- to 1½-inch-long double terminated clear quartz crystals on the forehead so that each connects the central crystal to one of the iolite or blue crystals on the temple.

9. Next, rest two blue calcites (or other light blue crystals) on the top of the head, each midway between the ears and the top of the crown. If terminated, point the tips away from the ears.

10. Now, begin to take long, deep, gentle breaths; relax the body as you do so.

11. Use a single terminated clear quartz crystal to trace an energy line from the crystal on the third eye to the amethyst on the crown chakra and upward past the clear crystals that surround the body. Then reverse the movement, tracing a pathway from above the crown center to the amethyst to the crystal on the third eye. Next, move your clear quartz crystal from one side of the head to the other, connecting the two iolite or royal blue crystals on the temples. Repeat this complete process for at least three minutes or longer. Focus on the third eye as you do so. If the process causes a headache, stop, soften the gaze on the third eye, and relax the forehead. When you feel ready, you can start again. There should never be any strain.

Chapter 10

CRYSTAL HEALING FOR COMMON MENTAL/EMOTIONAL AILMENTS

The body, mind, and emotions are all related and intertwined. The emotions are a function of the mind. You first make a mental decision and then have an emotional reaction. This likely causes another thought and another reactive emotion. These thoughts and feelings, in turn, affect your physical body—sometimes only slightly and other times quite a bit. For example, if you think that no one likes you, you might feel depressed. The depression causes you to feel lethargic and to take shallow breaths, which in turn, may affect your lungs or attract colds or the flu. An illness, in turn, may increase your depression, increasing your certainty that no one likes you. This loop of thoughts, emotions, and physical reactions can be endless and self-perpetuating.

When the body is out of balance, it is more likely than not that the mind and related emotions are, too. Because mental/emotional states are so often intertwined with physical ailments, healing one condition may heal the other.

Here are some specific techniques to heal common mental/emotional states that you are likely to encounter. These healings may help alleviate associated physical ailments as well.

ANGER

1. Place a rose quartz on the heart chakra. Surround it with four clear quartz crystals with their tips pointing outward.

2. Set a cooling green calcite on the abdominal third chakra (or, if the anger is strong, use green malachite). Place another green calcite or malachite on the belly button.

3. Lay a turquoise on the throat chakra and a cool blue calcite, celestite, or other light blue crystal on top of each jawbone.

4. Next, place black tourmaline or another black crystal about six inches below the feet, tip downward if terminated, to help draw anger out of the body.

5. Place a blue iolite, lapis, or other royal blue crystal on the third eye for insight.

6. Surround the body with cool green crystals, tips pointing outward if terminated.

7. Take long, deep breaths, feeling them flow in and out of the heart chakra. With every inhale, visualize a beautiful pink light entering the heart chakra. Relax with every exhale, imagining that the anger drains out from the bottom of your feet into the earth. Continue for as long as you like.

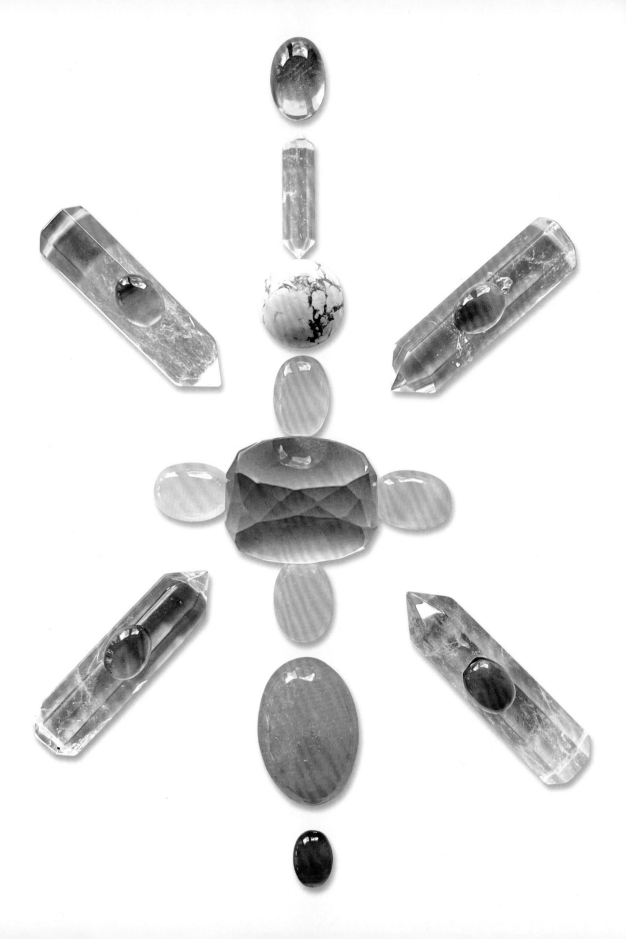

DEPRESSION

Depression can be understood as anger that turns inward toward the self instead of finding outward expression. It may also result from feelings of helplessness or loneliness, causing you to feel empty, gray, and lethargic. This crystal healing will uplift the mind and spirit.

1. Surround the body with light yellow calcite, citrine, or other clear, bright yellow crystals. If terminated, point the tips in toward the body. Use a single terminated clear quartz crystal to energetically connect these crystals and form a bright, yellow, energizing aura around the body.

2. Hold a rose quartz or other pink crystal in each hand.

3. Lay a rose quartz or other pink crystal on the heart chakra. Surround it with four smaller light green crystals. Imagine breathing in and out of this chakra, filling the heart, and then the body, with pink light. If the mind wanders, bring it back to your breathing and the loving, compassionate pink light. Do this for at least three minutes.

4. Next, place a bright yellow crystal on the navel point. Imagine your breath flowing in and out of this joyful yellow crystal. With every inhale, imagine its bright yellow light filling the body. Focus on this visualization for at least three minutes.

5. Now, place a white howlite or other opaque white crystal on the third eye to soothe the thinking mind. Place a selenite or double terminated clear quartz crystal on the crown chakra. Imagine that the breath flows in through the third eye and out through the crown. Then imagine that the breath flows in through the crown chakra and out through the third eye. Do this for at least three minutes.

6. Take long, deep, relaxing breaths. Imagine yourself floating within an aura of pink light that is surrounded with a bright, joyful yellow light. Do this for at least three minutes.

SHAME

Feelings of shame often result from old childhood wounds inflicted when your primary caretaker or parent withheld their love, treating you with contempt, as if you were innately deficient. Shame can also manifest in reaction to something wrong that you actually did or imagine you did. In either case, forgiveness is needed, for the early primary caretaker, for yourself and the wrong that you did, or for the imagined deficiency within you.

1. Surround the body with amethyst or violet crystals, their tips pointing inward if they are terminated. Place one crystal above the head, another below the feet, and evenly space one to three crystals along each side of the body. Visualize an aura of soft, violet, accepting, forgiving, healing light that surrounds the body.

2. Center two smoky quartz crystals or other brown stones on the bottoms of the feet. Place a black tourmaline or other black stone below, centered between the brown stones and still within the amethyst circle.

3. Hold an amethyst or violet crystal in each hand. If the crystals are terminated, point the tips toward the arms.

4. Next, place a pink kunzite, rose quartz, or other pink crystal on the heart chakra. Surround this with four green tourmaline or other green crystals: one above, one below, and one on each side. If terminated, point the tips in toward the heart chakra. Between each green crystal, place a white howlite or other calming opaque white stone.

5. Lay a green tourmaline, calcite, or other green crystal on the center of the belly.

6. Now, relax the body and focus on the heart center. Take long, deep breaths. On the inhale, imagine that the heart center expands and glows with a beautiful pink light. On the exhale, release all feelings of shame or unworthiness. Imagine that they leave through the bottoms of the feet and flow deep into the earth where they are then transformed into nurturing acceptance. Continue this for at least three minutes.

7. Next, focus on the heart center again, imagining the glowing pink light. Silently repeat these words: "I am good and honorable. I forgive myself and all who have harmed me. I am worthy of respect." Repeat these for at least three minutes, or until it seems like time to stop.

8. You may need to do this crystal healing process many times to attain its full effect. Try doing it as a thirty-day practice.

LOVE AND COMPASSION

Being in a state of love is different than being "in love." Living in a state of love is continual and enduring and doesn't depend on what is happening in your life. Being in love comes and goes, usually depending on the circumstances of your life. Though being in love is exciting as long as it lasts, living in a state of love is infinitely more satisfying. To reach this state, you must first accept yourself, accept others, and accept life as it is. Next, you must choose to focus on what satisfies your heart rather than concentrating on what is lacking, disappointing, or otherwise horrible. The goal is to stop being critical and, instead, be discriminating. When you live in a state of love, you tend to attract love to you, allowing you to maintain deeply fulfilling relationships.

The following crystal process will open you to a higher vision by expanding your understanding and your heart so that you are able to live in a state of deep and profound love.

1. Surround the body with alternating green tourmaline or other green crystals and rose quartz or other pink crystals. Use your single terminated clear quartz crystal to connect these stones and create a surrounding aura of pink and green light.

2. Surround the pink and green crystals with a ring of (preferably) double terminated clear quartz crystals, starting with one above the head. If the crystals are single terminated, point the tips in toward the body.

3. Place a sizeable single terminated amethyst on the crown chakra.

4. Place a Herkimer diamond that is at least 1¼ inch in height and width on the heart chakra. If no such diamond is available, then substitute a double terminated clear quartz crystal of at least 1½ inch in height and 1 inch in width. Before placing this crystal on the heart chakra, clear it, hold it in both hands, and program it with the highest, clearest, most loving and eternal energy of the universe.

5. Surround the heart center Herkimer diamond or clear quartz crystal with either green tourmaline or any other strong green crystal. Place one green crystal above the heart crystal, one below, and another on each side. If you wish to amplify this further, place smaller green crystals between the primary crystals and the heart crystal so that eight crystals surround the heart chakra stone.

6. Hold a violet crystal in each hand, tips pointing in toward the arms if they are single terminated.

7. Place a blue azurite, blue lapis, or other strong royal blue crystal on the third eye.

8. Once all of the crystals have been placed, take long, deep, breaths and relax the body. With each inhale, silently say the word *om (ohm)* while imagining your breath flowing in through the amethyst on the crown. With each exhale, silently say the word *ram (rahm)* while imagining your breath flowing out through the heart chakra crystal. Then reverse the process, imagining the breath flowing in through the heart chakra with the word *om* and out through the crown chakra with the word *ram*. Practice this meditation for at least seven minutes, though you may continue for as long as you like

9. Once you are finished with the previous step, focus on the heart chakra while silently repeating, "I am love." Continue this meditation for at least three minutes.

GRIEF

Grief is a normal response to the loss of someone or something that you love. As a healer, it is important to realize that grief has no schedule: There is no "right time" to move on from a loss. In fact, grief never really ends: It begins as intense pain and morphs into something more poignant and integral to who we are. Rather than trying to make grief disappear, then, the crystal healing should aim to transform intense pain into acceptance. That said, when someone's grief manifests as debilitating anguish, the crystal healing should seek to mitigate these feelings so that they become livable. When you perform your crystal healing, you want to provide loving support and assistance as you guide the bereaved to a state of peaceful acceptance. The crystal healing technique outlined below, which should prove helpful at all stages of grief, utilizes the symbolic walk through darkness to light.

1. Surround the body with amethyst crystals, their tips pointing outward if single terminated. Use a single terminated clear quartz crystal to connect the amethysts and form an aura of comforting, calming violet light.

2. Hold an amethyst crystal in each hand, tip pointing up toward the arms if single terminated.

3. Place a rose quartz in the heart center.

4. Relax the body and begin to take long, deep breaths. Imagine each breath flowing into and out of the heart chakra. Continue breathing in this way for at least three minutes.

5. Using the single terminated quartz crystal, sweep the surrounding violet aura toward and into the body. As you sweep, imagine that the body, mind, and heart are lovingly wrapped in a warm, comforting blanket of violet light. Let your body, mind, and emotions relax. Continue this process for at least three minutes.

6. Place a green calcite, green aventurine, or green malachite in the middle of the belly. Imagine that your long, deep breaths are now moving in and out of the crystal, relaxing and softening the belly as they go.

7. Place a soft yellow amber, yellow calcite, or any other soft yellow crystal on the third chakra.

8. Place a small cabochon-cut green malachite, jade, aventurine or other small, green stone on each closed eye.

9. Place a small soft blue calcite, kyanite, or other soft blue crystal on the throat chakra. Place additional soft blue crystals on each temple, on the jawbone, and on each side of the mouth.

10. Continue breathing with long, deep breaths. Feel your breath flowing into and out of the heart center. Let the chest and heart area relax with each breath.

11. Form a cross pattern by placing four small yellow citrines or other yellow crystals around the rose quartz on the heart center.

12. Use the single terminated quartz crystal to circle these heart crystals while visualizing a soft yet brilliant yellow light entering the heart center. With each breath, imagine that this yellow light flows into the heart center, eventually filling the entire body with golden light.

13. With every breath, imagine flowing upward into this golden light, eventually feeling as though you are one with the essence of light itself.

14. While sustaining this vision of golden light, silently repeat these words: "I am uplifted as I move from darkness to light." Continue repeating these words for at least three minutes. It is a good practice to repeat them during daily life.

15. Carry amethyst, rose quartz, and yellow citrine or other similarly colored crystals with you for a reminder of the walk from darkness to light.

FEAR AND PROTECTION

This crystal healing will help counter fear by providing a protective aura and feelings of security. The green crystal on the heart chakra will serve as a reminder that love, the ultimate source of all protection, is a much stronger energy than either hate or fear.

1. Place a green tourmaline or other green crystal on the heart chakra.

2. Surround the body with four, six, or eight black tourmaline crystals or other black crystals or stones (though black tourmaline is preferable). Place one above the head, another centered below the feet, and the rest at the sides of the body. Using a single terminated clear quartz crystal, energetically connect the black crystals so that they form a total protective aura around the body.

3. Place a red garnet, red tiger eye, red hematite, or other red crystal or stone at the base of the spine. Hold one red crystal or stone in each hand.

4. Place an orange carnelian or other bright orange crystal on the second chakra, about three inches below the belly button.

5. Place a yellow citrine or other bright yellow crystal on the third chakra, and another on the navel point.

6. Bring your focus to the red crystal at the base of the spine. Imagine that its energy flows upward into the body, bringing strength and security. Continuing this visualization, imagine the entire body filling with red light.

7. Envision whatever is feared. Imagine this fear approaching and meeting the black protective aura, where it is forcefully blasted away. Holding this vision in the mind's eye, take a deep inward breath and then powerfully blow it out. Imagine your breath carrying the fear away. Continue this visualization for at least three minutes, or keep going until the fear is removed. This exercise may be built into a thirty-day practice in order to banish more powerful fears.

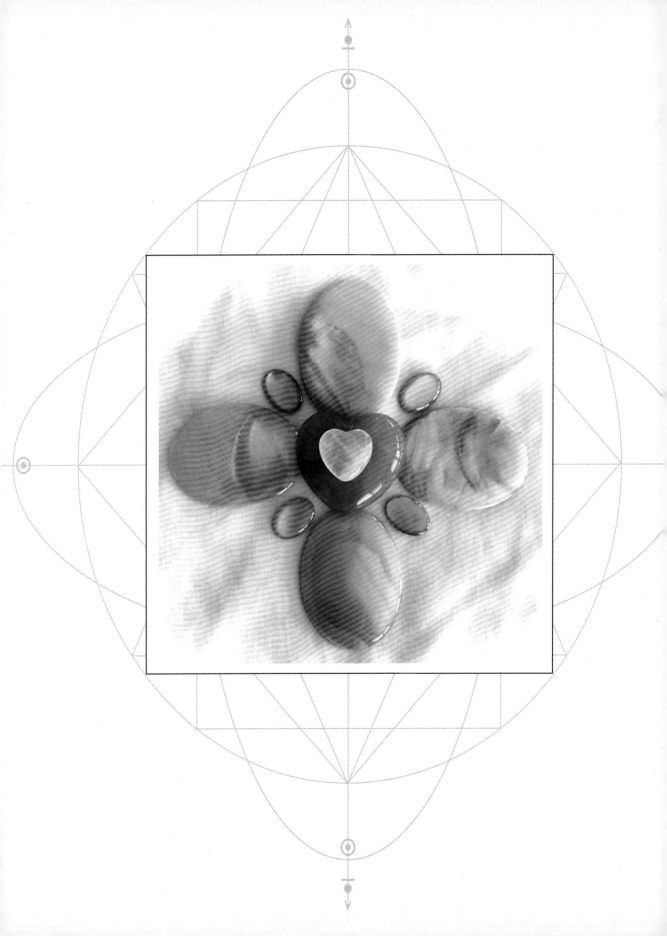

SUICIDE AND SELF-HARM

The desire to harm yourself or to end your life is a function of seemingly intolerable inner pain. The causes of cutting, anorexia, bulimia, and other forms of self-harm can be complicated, often stemming from early-childhood wounding, self-hatred, or extreme anxiety. Whatever the cause, self-harm is largely an attempt to stop inner pain when it seems as if there is no other way to do so. It is important to realize that anxiety and inner pain don't have to be based on reality. They may be based one's *perception of reality*, which can't be changed simply by denying its factual truth. Solutions to self-harm involve learning other ways of coping.

You can effectively work with suicidal ideation by focusing on the nature of the self. It is very powerful to ask a suicidal person, "Who is this self that you want to do away with? Can you describe this self? Can you picture it?" Not only does this shift the person's focus, but it helps them realize that because they can't really find or describe this self, they can't really kill it. This promotes an understanding that what they really want to do is stop the pain. Lessening the intensity of the inner pain and/or anxiety (or stopping it altogether) then becomes the healing work.

Once you have switched the focus from wanting to self-harm to wanting to alleviate inner suffering or overwhelming anxiety, you can use your crystals and stones to address the problem. Within the pages of this book, you will find many ways to calm and heal anxiety and other forms of emotional pain, all of which are usually intertwined with mental and physical symptoms. Sometimes knowing that someone really cares is all it takes for healing to begin.

NOTE: If a person talks about suicide, find out if they have a plan and the means to follow through on that plan. IF SO, IT IS ABSOLUTELY NECESSARY TO CALL 911 OR A SUICIDE HOTLINE. In fact, as a healer, you are mandated to do so.

This is true even if you are concerned about overreacting, worried about hurting the person's feelings, or afraid that you are wrong. None of that matters. It is better to be safe. You should also let the person's family and psychiatrist or therapist know. *You must always take this seriously.*

CHAPTER 11
BECOMING A MASTER CRYSTAL HEALER

If you practice the various healing techniques in this book, increasing your awareness of the higher planes of consciousness, becoming sensitive to subtle energy, and learning to harmonize and listen to your crystals, you will ultimately become a master crystal healer.

In this process, you may also develop other abilities beyond the physical senses and normal intuition. You may find yourself becoming clairvoyant, clairaudient, or psychic—attuned to the information and realities on other planes of existence. You may be able to read someone's thoughts and their feelings without being told. You will be able to tell where other people are experiencing mental, emotional, and physical pain and how it is manifesting in them. As you become sensitized, you may well be able to feel vibrations in objects, people, and an entire environment—even from afar or simply from seeing a picture. You may be able to view the past or the future. Your dreams may become so lucid that they seem to be just as real as your everyday life. You may be able to experience the self in a way that extends well beyond your thoughts, emotions, or your physical body. You may encounter a self that is formless and endless, unaffected even by death.

If or when these abilities or states of awareness start happening, it is easy to get lost in them, thinking that they make you more important and special than other people. It is vitally important, then, that you view these abilities as mere signposts along the road, providing a signal that you are on the path to becoming a good crystal healer. If you start thinking of yourself as superior to other people, you have taken a wrong turn and are focusing on the limited ego-self rather than the unlimited self. The more you focus on the limited ego-self, the more your healing abilities are likely to dry up and even end entirely.

The most wonderful thing about your journey to becoming a master crystal healer is that you will eventually be able to live a totally satisfying and joyful life. Your heart will be able to hold a magnitude of love that is endless in its capacity. Not only will you be able to share your healing abilities with others, but in the process of this sharing, you will also be able to partake in a vast loving and compassionate presence that exists without measure or end.

I wish you well on your crystal healing journey. May it bring you satisfaction and great peace. May you be successful and effective as a true crystal healer. May the wisdom of the ages be yours, and may you become one with the blissful wonder of infinite awareness.

OM SHANTI
MAY YOU BE HAPPY.

INDEX

MANDALA

An imprint of MandalaEarth

PO Box 3088 San Rafael, CA 94912

www.MandalaEarth.com

Find us on Facebook: www.Facebook.com/MandalaEarth

Follow us on Twitter: @MandalaEarth

Library of Congress Cataloging-in-Publication Data available.

ISBN: 978-1-64722-417-2

Publisher: Raoul Goff
Associate Publisher: Phillip Jones
Creative Director: Chrissy Kwasnik
Associate Art Director: Ashley Quackenbush
Design Support: Brooke McCullum
Editorial Director: Katie Killebrew
Managing Editor: Matt Wise
Editorial Assistant: Sophia Wright
Senior Production Manager: Greg Steffen

Photos by: Uma Silbey
Additional photos: Shutterstock: pages 2, 4, 6, 8, 14, 18, 24, 27, 40, 43, 48, 51, 56, 80, 90, 118, 141, 142, 174, 191, 192, 197, 208, 264, 267.
Models: Taryn Kama Givenchy and Leah Francisco

ROOTS of PEACE   REPLANTED PAPER

Earth Aware Editions, in association with Roots of Peace, will plant two trees for each tree used in the manufacturing of this book. Roots of Peace is an internationally renowned humanitarian organization dedicated to eradicating land mines worldwide and converting war-torn lands into productive farms and wildlife habitats. Roots of Peace will plant two million fruit and nut trees in Afghanistan and provide farmers there with the skills and support necessary for sustainable land use.

Manufactured in China by Insight Editions

10 9 8 7 6 5 4 3 2